Praise for *Mindful Emotion*

Buy this book, read it, practise with it. It's a wonderfully welcome addition to the body of work around mindfulness and compassion. It's engaging, down-to-earth but uplifting, and very much to the point.

The authors come across as kindly but never sentimental and their book extends the conversation around mindfulness – and its practice – into further, and much needed, domains.

I'll certainly be recommending it to all those who have attended my mindfulness classes.

Michael Chaskalson, author of *Mindfulness in Eight Weeks*

Mindful Emotion: A Short Course in Kindness is a stimulating guide and training program that uses the analogy of cultivating a garden that results in the finest flowers and fruits to illustrate the process of cultivating kindness toward others. A variety of secular-based mindfulness meditation instructions and thoughtful exercises support this process of creating a garden of kindness, which is what our world so badly needs right now.

Bhikshuni Thubten Chodron, author of *Good Karma: How to Create the Causes of Happiness and Avoid the Causes of Suffering*

The last 20 years has seen research showing us that what motivates us also patterns our minds and bodies. While modern societies encourage self-focused competitiveness, ancient wisdoms point to the importance of caring, helping, supporting, kindness and compassion for self and others as the true path to happiness and well-being. This deeply informative book brings together secular science, ancient wisdoms and psychotherapeutic insights, in a series of steps and practices to cultivate kindness to self and others and thereby reap its benefits. Accessible and practical, this book will be of great benefit to many.

Professor Paul Gilbert, PhD, FBPsS, OBE, author of *The Compassionate Mind*

With the problems we face in today's world, kindness is more important than ever. In *Mindful Emotion*, the authors have produced a thorough and pragmatic guide to bringing mindfulness and kindness into our lives. It is an excellent book that I will be recommending to colleagues, clients, and friends.

Russell Kolts, Ph.D., Professor of Psychology at Eastern Washington University and author of *CFT Made Simple: A Clinician's Guide to Practicing Compassion-Focused Therapy*

The benefits of mindfulness are so much greater when they include a focus on kindness and compassion, both for ourselves and others. This book is a wonderful journey through the art and practice of mindful kindness – or as I like to call it, Kindfulness.

Dr Mark Williamson, Director of Action for Happiness

Mindful Emotion

A Short Course in Kindness

*Dr Paramabandhu Groves
and Dr Jed Shamel*

indhorse Publications

Windhorse Publications
169 Mill Road
Cambridge
CB1 3AN
UK

info@windhorsepublications.com
windhorsepublications.com

Cover design by Dhammarati

Typesetting and layout by Ruth Rudd
Printed by Bell & Bain Ltd, Glasgow

British Library Cataloguing in Publication Data:

A catalogue record for this book is available from the British Library.

ISBN: 978 1 909314 70 2

Dedication

The book is dedicated to the loving memory of Talal Shamel.

Contents

Audio downloads

This book has been produced with accompanying guided meditations and reflections by the authors, available as free downloads. They can be streamed directly from the Web or downloaded in MP3 format. Please go to bit.ly/meaudio, windhorsepublications.com/mindful-emotion-audio, or kindnessbehaviourtraining.com.

Authors' acknowledgements

We thank the many people who have supported and assisted in this book. We developed the course at Breathing Space in London and appreciate the participation and feedback from course participants. Priyananda, Michelle Bernard and Giulietta Spudich from Windhorse Publications have been very supportive in backing the idea for the book and seeing it through to publication. Cynthia Troup provided excellent editorial guidance, and Lisa Dutheil gave helpful feedback on an early draft. Finally, many thanks to Maitreyabandhu, who had the original idea for the KBT course and encouraged us to write the book.

Publisher's acknowledgements

Windhorse Publications wishes to gratefully acknowledge a grant from the Triratna European Chairs' Assembly Fund and the Future Dharma Fund towards the production of this book.

Windhorse Publications also wishes to gratefully acknowledge and thank the individual donors who gave to the book's production via our 'Sponsor-a-book' campaign.

Introduction

....

Germination

Three things in human life are important. The first is to be kind. The second is to be kind. The third is to be kind.

Henry James

Origins and the mindfulness explosion

'I'm not managing to do all my home practice. Still, I suppose just going along to the mindfulness course is helpful.' The person listening nods in agreement. Overhearing conversations like this on public transport and in restaurants has become less and less remarkable. While we were writing this book, *Mindful Nation UK*, a report by the Mindfulness All-Party Parliamentary Group, was published by the UK government, perhaps indicating just how popular the interest in mindfulness has become.

Mindfulness has a long pedigree of practice in the Buddhist tradition. At the London Buddhist Centre we started teaching mindfulness in therapeutic courses in 2004, initially for depression and then for addiction and stress. One of the issues that soon emerged from teaching courses such as Mindfulness-Based Cognitive Therapy (MBCT) for depression was not only the struggle to do the home practice, as the unknown passenger on the London Underground was describing above, but also how to keep mindfulness practice alive after the eight-week course had finished.

Going back to the Buddhist tradition for inspiration, we have recognized that the most obvious missing element from mindfulness courses such as MBCT is kindness – not that kindness is completely absent from such courses. The quality of awareness that one is trying to develop with mindfulness is one imbued with kindness; and as teachers, we try to

....

embody kindness in our approach to teaching. Nevertheless, the direct development of kindness is not usually a major part of mindfulness-based courses. While some teachers of mindfulness believe this is sufficient, others feel there is a role for the active cultivation of kindness. Indeed, there is evidence to suggest that one of the factors determining whether or not someone has a successful outcome in MBCT is their ability to cultivate mindfulness of a kindly nature.

In the wake of and alongside the mindfulness explosion, there has been a smaller but growing interest in the development of kindness and compassion. Examples of this include Compassion Focused Therapy (CFT), the work of Paul Gilbert, and Mindful Self-Compassion, developed in particular by Kristin Neff and Christopher Germer. The main emphasis in these approaches is on *self*-compassion. Given how much many people struggle with negative attitudes towards themselves, emphasizing self-compassion has made sense. Even so, in revisiting Buddhist meditative practices we find that kindness is cultivated both towards self *and* others. Therefore we decided to create a course in kindness rooted in the Buddhist tradition and inspired by contemporary compassion and mindfulness approaches, especially Acceptance and Commitment Therapy and CFT.

Why self and other?

1. Leaving no stone unturned
The principal Buddhist meditation on kindness, called *mettā bhāvanā* in Pali (*maitrī* in Sanskrit), has five stages. Kindness is cultivated in turn towards oneself, a friend, a person one doesn't have strong like or dislike for, a person one is having difficulty with, and all beings. We are using the framework of these five stages, as they enable working with the full range of our basic emotional responses: like, dislike, and indifference. Our aim, ambitious perhaps, is to be able respond with kindness in all situations. Kindness is barely worth the name if it dissolves in the face of the first difficulty encountered such as a curt shop

assistant or a teenager having a strop. We want kindness that is robust and able to respond creatively to whatever life throws at us.

2. Easier to be kind to a friend
Bringing to mind an attitude of kindness towards a friend often occurs easily and spontaneously, in contrast to the struggle we can have in being kind towards ourself. For this reason, we sometimes swap the first two stages round, starting with a friend to create a mood of well-wishing and kindness.

3. Going beyond self-preoccupation
Attending to others, in addition to ourself, can help to balance an unhelpful over-preoccupation with 'me'. The culture of consumerism in technologically advanced, rich countries has led to increasing social isolation and fragmentation. Retail therapy, just a click away, fills the vacuum left by the retreat of religion (or competes with it) and promotes a focus on getting and spending. To look beyond the unhealthy obsession with self can be refreshing. Concern for others brings a broader perspective to alleviate the burden of self-preoccupation.

4. Not excluding oneself
At the same time, we are not recommending ignoring our own needs and desires. The balance can tip unhealthily towards self-abnegation. This can stem from cultural conditioning to put the needs of others first. Negative attitudes towards ourself can also come from unrealistic expectations of ourself, often a symptom of unhelpful excessive self-preoccupation. Cultivating kindness can counter and transform negative self-views.

5. Interconnectedness
Eventually we can go beyond thinking in terms of self or other. The world we live in is deeply interconnected. We affect one another all the time and depend on each other for our very survival, although this is easy to forget in our atomized lives. Examined closely, the boundaries of self and other break down. Kindness fully developed encompasses all. We can learn the

wisdom of realizing our interdependence through cultivating kindness towards both ourself and others.

Kindness Behaviour Training

We have called the course Kindness Behaviour Training (KBT). We chose kindness rather than compassion, as the latter primarily implies a response to suffering. Although we could all be considered to suffer on a fundamental, existential level, daily life brings moments of joy and pleasure as well as pain and suffering. Kindness is a response to whatever is happening, whether pleasant, painful, or indifferent. The word 'kind', going back to Old English, has been in the English language for longer than the Latinate word 'compassion'. 'Kindness' is not as big a word as 'compassion', and is perhaps more approachable. We may be able to imagine performing small acts of kindness more readily than being compassionate. Kindness is like a road: it can take us on a long journey that in time may have far-reaching consequences and embrace other qualities such as compassion, but it has the advantage of starting right outside our front door. Starting from where we are now, we can practise being a little kinder in our life.

The behaviour part of KBT is a reminder that kindness is something we can do. Although we use meditation as a vehicle for working with our mind, kindness in KBT is not simply about enjoying fuzzy warm feelings with our eyes closed. Indeed nice feelings, in the sense of a pleasant glow, are definitely a secondary consideration. KBT is a call to action. We work on our mind to augment our motivation so that we can be kinder in our speech and action. Acting with kindness will make it easier to cultivate kind states of mind. Meditation and action mutually reinforce each other. The overarching aim is to act with kindness, open-heartedness, and generosity.

KBT is a training because it requires practice. Like any valuable life skill, it is something we can learn to embrace more fully and get better at. As we practise, we see more and more subtle and skilful ways of acting with kindness. We learn to combat the unhelpful ingrained habits of our heart and to transform them into ways of being that benefit both us and others and harvest rich rewards.

Who is KBT for?

KBT was first developed as a follow-on course for those who had completed a course in mindfulness, especially one of the therapeutic mindfulness courses such as MBCT for depression, mindfulness-based stress reduction, or mindfulness-based addiction recovery. KBT is a great way to take further and expand on what has been learnt on a mindfulness course, whether secular or Buddhist. But experience of mindfulness is not assumed, as the first two weeks of a KBT course give a basic grounding in mindfulness. Essentially, KBT is for anyone who values kindness and wishes to bring more kindness into their life.

Mindful emotion

Mindful Emotion: A Short Course in Kindness is the coursebook for KBT. We use the term 'mindful emotion' in two ways. Firstly, we are trying to become mindful of our emotional life. Mindfulness encompasses becoming aware of all aspects of our experience: body sensations, thoughts and emotions, and the world around us. Becoming mindful of our emotions is especially important because, as the word implies, it is our emotions that move us. The word 'emotion' comes from the Old French *esmovoir*, to excite, which comes from the Latin *ēmovēre*, to disturb; it is ultimately derived from the Latin *movēre*, to move. So emotions disturb and excite us as well as move us, and they are also what motivate us. Yet often either we are not so aware of our emotions (and thus of what is moving us) or our emotions are unruly and even destructive. Our starting point, then, is to become aware of what our emotions are. In particular, we learn to notice more fully emotional responses to ourself, to our friends, to people we have difficulty with, and to the large swathe of people who don't elicit a strong emotional response but form the backdrop of our life.

Secondly, by mindful emotion we mean emotion that has been tended to with wise and careful attention, with mindfulness. It is as though we have been given charge of a new garden – first of all we need to find out what is growing. We need to see what will germinate in the soil. So with the garden of our mind: we need to become aware of our existing emotional habits, the sort of emotions that tend to arise, the seeds that have been planted through events and actions in the past. Once we know what is already growing, we can start to shape the garden. We can decide what we want to cultivate and what to weed out in order to create something harmonious and beautiful. In the heart's garden, our aim is to sow the seeds of happiness so as to produce the finest flowers and fruit, and chief among these is kindness.

How to use this book

You can read through *Mindful Emotion* and follow the course at your own rate, using the exercises as suggested. Alternatively you can dip into the book and read topics that interest you or do the exercises that catch your attention. The eight chapters cover the eight weeks of the course. The first two chapters are on mindfulness. This will act as an introduction to mindfulness for those unfamiliar with practising it and as a refresher for those who are familiar with mindfulness practice. In order to give more information to those who are relatively new to mindfulness, the first chapter covers much important ground and is longer than the subsequent chapters. The rest of the course discusses six different ways to approach kindness in meditation and how to act with kindness in our daily life. The six approaches are:

1. Using words and phrases (Chapter 3)
2. Using the breath (Chapter 4)
3. Gratitude (Chapter 5)
4. Using imagination (Chapter 6)
5. Common humanity (Chapter 7)
6. Kindness in the universe (Chapter 8)

Mindful Emotion

There is no one way of cultivating kindness that suits all, so we encourage you to experiment with the different approaches and not to be disheartened if one or more don't seem to get you anywhere. Cultivating kindness is a creative process, and these approaches are not exhaustive. How we respond to different approaches is likely to change over time. As you become more used to the approaches, you may find that you want to combine them, for example holding an anchor of the breath while reflecting on our common humanity.

Chapter 3 goes into much more detail about what we mean by kindness. We explore masks and hurdles, things that get in the way of cultivating authentic kindness. We introduce the kindness breathing space, which is a bridge to bring kindness cultivated in meditation into our day-to-day life. In Chapter 4, we look at some of the science behind kindness, especially in terms of evolutionary psychology. Acting with kindness is brought out more in the remaining chapters, through generosity (Chapter 5) and contentment (Chapter 6) and in our speech (Chapter 7). In Chapter 8, we tackle the difficult but important topic of forgiveness.

Throughout the book, there are extra tips for working in meditation. As people often struggle with developing kindness towards themselves, we have included extra advice on working with this tricky first stage of kindness meditation. If you are getting stuck with meditation or find difficulties arising (especially if you have experienced trauma in the past), you can find additional help in Appendix 1: Kindness meditation: Staying creative.

Each chapter has a main meditation that we recommend you practise; we call it the core meditation. There are also some supplementary or bonus meditations, which complement the core meditation or sometimes may be an alternative to it. In addition, you will find some guided reflections and written tasks to help you engage with the material being covered. The different sorts of exercises are indicated with icons as follows:

Core meditation

 Bonus meditation

 Guided reflection

 Written task

Research reading and findings

If we have found studies that illuminate the topic we are discussing, we have included their details so that you can consult them. During the development of KBT, we conducted a study to learn how people found the course. We have included some of their comments in order to give you an idea of what it was like doing KBT and of some of the effects that practising KBT had on their life. You will find them in Appendix 3.

Home practice and downloads

At the end of each of the eight chapters, there are suggestions for home practice. If you are following the book as a course, these are the practices that we would recommend you to do between each chapter. KBT is, as its name indicates, a training, and so in general the more practice, the better. However, there is no point in giving yourself a hard time if you don't do the home practices or don't do them very regularly. It would be a shame if a book on kindness were to become a stick to beat yourself with!

To help with the practices as well as the written instructions in the book, all meditations and guided reflections are available as audio downloads. You can download them and additional information, including practice sheets, from our website at kindnessbehaviourtraining.com and see p. ix.

Chapter one

....

Preparing the earth

The moment one gives close attention to anything, even a blade of grass, it becomes a mysterious, awesome, indescribably magnificent world in itself.

Henry Miller

At a glance

- Mindfulness is the foundation for cultivating kindness.
- We can distinguish mindfulness from automatic pilot.
- Aspects of mindfulness include an attitude of curiosity and discerning wisely.
- We can develop mindfulness through informal practices such as mindful walking and through formal meditations such as mindfulness of breath and body.
- Having a daily meditation practice is very helpful, and it is worth considering what factors support this.
- Recognizing what mindfulness is *not* can help to prevent unnecessary disappointments and problems.

Seeds have enormous variety. Some, like those of the oak and the chestnut, are relatively large; others, such as those of orchids, are almost as small as dust. Some have means to help propel them in the wind such as the hair of a dandelion or the keys of an ash. Others have little hooks, like the burrs of the dock plant, which are dispersed by attaching themselves to fur or feathers, or they have a fleshy covering, like apples, that entice animals. They usually have some food reserves that help the young plant to get started. But, whatever the variety, they all need favourable conditions, such as warmth and moisture and a medium such as soil, in which to grow.

Like the many different types of seed, there are many ways to cultivate kindness, and this book will introduce us to a selection of approaches. Our impulses to generate kindness, like the nutrients in a seed, can get us going, but only so far; and without the correct conditions, and especially without a favourable medium in which to grow, our impulses, like seedlings, will wither and die. If you have ever tried to grow something from seed, you will have made some effort to provide a medium in which to grow the plants, whether that has been to clear weeds from a patch of earth, to open a bag of potting compost, or to moisten some paper towel for mustard and cress.

The medium from which kindness grows is mindfulness. The more attention we give to preparing our mind and heart through mindfulness, the richer our harvest of kindness. Cress for egg sandwiches works with blotting paper because we only need the baby leaves. For a good crop of potatoes or plums from a tree, we need well-prepared earth. In this chapter and the one that follows, we shall explore how to develop mindfulness in order to support and sustain the cultivation of kindness.

What is mindfulness?

The basic element of mindfulness is to pay attention. Mindfulness is like a spotlight that shines on the object of our attention, enabling us to see and know the object. We can distinguish mindfulness from automatic pilot. Automatic pilot is a very useful function of the mind that enables us to carry out activities without having to give them much conscious attention. If we hear the phone ring in the next room, we can get up, walk to the other room, opening the door as we go, all the while wondering if that is our friend getting back to us and what we are going to say to them, without giving any thought to how we use our body to get there. When we are learning to drive a car or to ride a bike, it can be quite a struggle and require lots of attention and concentration.

But, once we have acquired the skills, we can operate the car or bicycle with little thought of how to do so and instead give our attention to having a conversation with someone or perhaps singing a song. Just as we can perform many body actions without giving much attention to them, so many mental processes operate without much attention from us. For example, we might have a conversation about a film with someone and find that we can't remember the name of the principal actor. We struggle to recollect his name and then give up. The conversation continues and, twenty minutes later, the actor's name pops up in our mind. It is as though the mind has been working on the problem in the background and then furnishes us with the answer at a later time.

The ability to be able to carry out many body and mental functions without much conscious awareness is essential to going about our life, but it can also cause problems. Sometimes it can be just a minor inconvenience, as when we intend to stop at the supermarket on the way home from work and realize that we have missed the turning because we were on automatic pilot heading straight for home. Or we forget that our back is a bit delicate and bend carelessly, causing a flare-up of pain.

Large portions of our mental processes can proceed on automatic pilot. For example, someone is a bit sharp with us at work and we don't register that it upset us because we are trying to get on with writing a report. Without realizing this, it puts us in a slightly bad mood that colours our day and sets off in the background a story of disgruntlement. Other, perhaps neutral events are filtered through this lens, making our colleagues, who are also busy and feeling under pressure, seem unfriendly. This builds up in the background of our mind, so that when we come home, we snap at our partner over some trivial disagreement that quickly blows up into a row. We may not even remember the triggering event, but our mind has been swept along well-worn paths.

In automatic pilot, or mindlessness, our mind will tend to do whatever it is used to doing. If our habit is to criticize ourself or if it is to blame other people, then that is what we shall do. Like channels cut deeper by flood water or shortcuts across lawns that become muddy with increasing footfall, our mind develops habits that get stronger through repeated use. When habits are unhelpful, automatic pilot, by running them as a default, will exacerbate our suffering.

Automatic pilot does not seem like a problem when the story we are telling ourself is pleasurable and light, but sometimes it's scary and even terrifying. Like a film playing in our head, sometimes we get absorbed in the plot and sometimes we want to get up and leave. When we are preoccupied with the film, it is as though our attention is taken hostage by our suffering. Mindfulness is about knowing where our mind is from moment to moment and directing our attention in more creative ways.

By deliberately paying attention to what is going on, mindfulness can help us to see our habitual patterns and to step out of being caught up in them. Mindfulness is like coming to our senses or coming round after sleep. The activity of mindfulness is to repeatedly come to. Even though we keep getting caught up in our thoughts and feelings, sucked into automatic pilot, we can develop the habit of remembering to come into awareness, so that our thoughts and emotions are not left unchecked for too long.

Like a mother gazing lovingly at her child, we need to develop an attitude of open-heartedness and warmth to our unchecked emotions. This is the spirit of mindfulness in which we approach our efforts. It's not possible to be aware of anything for very long if we stare at it with disgust and judgement.

Research box: Distraction

Distraction is common, and usually does not conduce to happiness. A study used an iPhone app to ask more than 2,000 people how they were feeling at the moment they read the message and whether or not they were thinking about something other than what they were doing. Mind wandering occurred almost half the time, and people reported generally being less happy when their mind was wandering .[1]

Guided reflection: A mindful moment (three minutes)

Pause now for a moment, less than a minute. Having read the following paragraph (or listened to it on the website), we invite you to put down the book and try this exercise.

Find a place to sit (if you are not already sitting down) and notice the contact with the chair. Feel the weight of your body being supported by the chair. Feel your feet on the ground. How does your body feel? Is it light or heavy? Is it tired or energized? Notice that you are breathing and pay attention to where you are breathing most strongly. Perhaps it is strongest around the nostrils, the chest rising and falling, or perhaps in the abdomen as the belly expands and contracts with each breath. Gently explore your body and discover where your breathing is easiest to notice.

Does your breath feel smooth and regular or is it more jerky? Are the breaths shallow or deep? Really try to feel the sensations of the breathing. Allow yourself to follow a few breaths as they enter and leave the body. When you notice that your mind has wandered off, as it inevitably will, simply return to noticing the rhythm of your breath.

Notice how you are feeling. Are you feeling happy or sad? Are you bored, upset, excited, irritable or are you content? Or are you not feeling anything in particular? See if you can notice your thoughts. Are there any worries or preoccupations on your mind? What is the landscape of your mind like? Is it heavy, busy, or light and spacious? How does this way of attending to your experience compare with your everyday awareness of experience during your usual activities?

Non-judgement, discernment, and choosing

Usually, contemporary writings on mindfulness emphasize that mindfulness is non-judgemental. This points to an important aspect of mindfulness: we easily tend to be unhelpfully critical of ourself and our experience. For example, we might notice that we are having angry thoughts about someone, and then we harshly criticize ourself for having those angry thoughts. Or we are sitting in meditation and notice that our mind is distracted. It keeps wandering off to thoughts about who we are meeting for lunch or the film we saw last night, and we feel critical of our mind for not being more still. In both cases, the negative judging of our experience is counterproductive and only adds to our suffering.

An attitude of curiosity

Instead of making negative judgements, we aim to bring an attitude of interest to whatever arises. So whenever we become aware of something – our thoughts, emotions, or body sensations – we try, first of all, to be curious about the experience. Even if what we become aware of is critical, judging thoughts, we try to take an interest in them. Thus our starting point as we turn the spotlight of awareness onto something is simply to notice and recognize what is going on. We don't jump in with an attempt to fix it or tell ourself that we shouldn't be having this experience. What is happening is happening; it has already come into being.

This, of course, isn't always easy. We have strong habits of judging – I like this, I don't like that – and all the thoughts and emotions that proliferate from these preferences are woven into the fabric of our basic make-up. Part of the process of mindfulness is recognizing just how much judging we do, often on automatic pilot, and learning not to react to it with more criticism. Also, our feelings can be so strong at times, particularly if they are painful, that it can be hard not to immediately just wish the experience away.

Choosing how to respond

But once we do pay full attention with interest to something, the attitude of non-judgement does not mean that we don't evaluate and make choices. With the example of having angry thoughts about someone, we don't need to negatively criticize ourself for having those thoughts. Nevertheless, mindfulness includes an element of knowing or discernment, and it may become quickly apparent that our angry thoughts are both painful and unhelpful. With that knowledge, we can then choose how best to respond to those thoughts. It might be that just seeing their painful quality is enough for us to let them go, but we might need to work more actively – indeed we might decide the best thing to do is to include the person we are angry with in a kindness meditation (which we shall be exploring in much of the rest of the book).

Choosing where to attend

Another area of choice is deciding where we put our attention. For example, sitting in meditation, we might notice that our knee is painful. On the one hand, it would probably be unhelpful to completely ignore the pain, pretending it's not happening. We might be able to make a slight adjustment that eases the discomfort; and even if we can't alleviate the pain through a small movement, wilfully ignoring the discomfort is likely to have an adverse effect on our mind and to make us more tense. On the other hand, we don't need to spend the whole meditation focusing on our painful knee. We can acknowledge it and then give our attention to other parts of the body. We may find that, while our knee is painful, we have a warm, relaxed feeling in the shoulders. This can bring a perspective to our experience, leading to greater balance and even-mindedness.

Learning to choose where we put our attention can also help with our emotions. Suppose we are feeling angry about an email we received. We can easily find ourself being sucked into a maelstrom of irritation with its spiky thoughts as we replay our hard-done-by story or try to push it out of our mind, ignoring it, only to create tension in our neck and face. Instead we can acknowledge the annoyance, maybe feel the energy it contains, and then give our attention to something else, perhaps to the sensation of our feet on the ground or the sights in front of us, taking in the colours and shapes. We may move back and forth, attending to the anger and how it is affecting the body for a while, moving to the contact of the ground beneath our feet, and then back to noticing the anger again.

We can also choose to broaden or to narrow the focus of our awareness, like a torch that has a beam you can focus or spread out. In the examples above, we might choose to focus closely for a while on the pain in the knee or the qualities of the angry mind, or we might decide to broaden our awareness to include the whole body or even the total field of mental and physical sensations that are arising in that moment. In this way, the pain or anger is held within a bigger space of attention and so becomes less overwhelming or all-consuming.

Part of the skill of mindfulness is getting to know how best to respond to our experience. We learn, often through trial and error, to judge when best to give something more focused attention and when to broaden our awareness or to put our attention elsewhere. We start to recognize sticky thoughts and emotions that we easily get unhelpfully caught up in and we find ways to respond more creatively to them. Mindfulness of breath and body is a good way to learn some of these skills.

Greet and choose

We can summarize the overall thrust of mindfulness as a two-stage activity: greeting and choosing. Firstly, we greet whatever arises in our awareness with a sense of welcoming, like a good friend who has travelled a long way to visit us. Even if what shows up is boring, such as the umpteenth mental rerun of tomorrow's shopping list, or unpleasant, like the arising of a feeling of envy, we still greet it in a friendly way. We do this in order not to get into fighting or struggling with our experience or to be subtly pushing it away. All these types of aversion will create tension in our body and mind.

Secondly, we choose where to go with what has arisen. When we greet what has arisen, attention with friendly awareness may be sufficient to allow us to let it go. The process can be supported by the breath. We can greet with the in-breath and let go with the out-breath. Alternatively, we may decide to go into what has arisen more fully (something we shall explore more in the next chapter) or to go somewhere else with our attention, broadening it out or putting it elsewhere.

Core Meditation 1: Mindfulness of breath and body (fifteen minutes)

The mind needs a hook or a foothold. Most of our mental suffering arises when we are jumping from one thought or subject to another without direction. We feel either preoccupied with unhelpful thoughts or exhausted by the sheer pace and intensity of the feelings in our body. So we need to give our mind an anchor, a neutral place to go. The most common and easily accessible anchor for our mind is our breath and body.

Breathing is continuous, twenty-four hours a day, and it's familiar and easy to notice because it creates a slight movement in the body. It's our most loyal friend, accompanying us from birth to death.

In this meditation, we pay attention to the sensations of the breath and then to any sensations in the body. We try as best we can to really feel those sensations – just what they are like and where they appear in the body. Our mind will tend to wander away from the breath and body, for example getting caught up in fantasies or worries about the future. Noticing where our mind heads off to allows us to start recognizing its habitual patterns. Once we realize our mind has wandered off, we simply note where it has gone and then return our attention to the breath or body.

Meditation can be done sitting on a chair, on cushions, or on a meditation stool. We try to be as comfortable as possible. We want to have the lower body stable, supported by the ground and our chair or cushion while having the upper body upright without tensing up. It can also be done lying down, especially if you have chronic pain, although there is a greater risk of falling asleep.

Preparation

First of all, we scan our body. Start by feeling the contact of your feet on the ground. Notice the temperature of your feet and the sensations of any footwear. Gradually move your awareness up your legs. Notice if there is any holding on, especially in the thighs. Allow yourself to feel your body in contact with the clothes you are wearing and in contact with the seat you are sitting or the surface you are lying on. Become aware of your torso, your back, and your spine. If you are sitting up, feel the natural curves of the spine rising out of the pelvis; and if you are lying down, feel your spine being supported by the ground. Notice any sensations in your neck, head, and face. Is there any tightness in the face? If you can, allow the face to soften. Notice your shoulders. Is there any tension there? Take awareness to your arms and hands. If you are sitting up, check that your hands are supported by your lap so that you can let go of the arms.

Now notice your breathing. Feel the chest and perhaps the belly expanding and contracting. Be aware of how you are feeling. Note if you feel happy or sad, bored or excited, content or irritated, some other emotion, or perhaps nothing in particular.

Stage one: The breath

Without trying to change your breath in any way, allow yourself to follow its movements in and out of the body. Become interested in just what the breath is like: deep or shallow, long or short, smooth or irregular.

Sooner or later, your mind will wander away from the breath. That's just what minds do. When you become aware that your mind has wandered off, use this as an opportunity to notice where it has gone. Note what has taken up your attention. Notice how you are feeling, what emotions are present. If you have been caught up in something that is uncomfortable or painful, just note that discomfort is present and see if you can let go of the story or thoughts about the discomfort. Once you have noted where your mind has gone, gently bring your attention back to the breathing.

Stage two: The body

Now broaden your awareness to notice any sensations arising in the body. You might, for example, notice contact with the ground, the sensation of clothing resting on your skin, one part of the body touching another, or internal sensations. As best you can, be interested in just what the sensations are like. Are they sharp or dull, changing quickly, or more sustained? Just where in the body can you feel them? Again and again, each time the mind wanders off, note where it has gone to, what emotions are present and then return gently to the body sensations.

When you are ready, bring the meditation to a close. Pause a little before getting up and then perhaps stretch your body before continuing with your day.

Formal and informal practices

With formal mindfulness practices such as mindfulness of breath and body meditation, we set aside time to systematically cultivate mindfulness. Whether that is ten or twenty minutes, an hour, or even more, our sole aim is learning to be more mindful. It is like being in the laboratory, where we have more controlled conditions. Doing breath and body meditation, we give our attention to noticing body sensations, recognizing when our mind wanders off and coming back to the breath or body. Formal practice helps us to live with discomfort, to inhabit our bodies in a way that allows a spacious field for our emotions and sensations to be felt and explored. It helps us to cultivate the freedom to respond rather than to react. That's all we have to do. Of course that can be difficult enough; but during formal meditation, we are not trying to drive a car through an unfamiliar town, negotiate with our bank manager or the housing department, or get the children off to school. The laboratory of formal meditation practice allows us to develop our mindfulness skills in easier conditions.

Formal practice is never an end in itself. However, we don't want to be mindful only when we are sitting on a cushion. We want the benefits of being mindful in the rest of our daily life too. And that's where informal practices come in. By deliberately trying to be more mindful during simple activities, we can bridge the gap between formal practice and the rest of our life. Even without informal practices, if we are setting aside time each day to meditate, the effects are likely to spill over to other parts of our life. We might find ourself being more mindful at work or in talking with our family. In the middle of a heated discussion, for example, we might come to recognize that we are off on one of our familiar patterns. Informal practices make the transition from what we learn in sitting meditation to daily life more likely.

In principle, we can be mindful while doing any activity; but with informal practices, we choose a relatively simple activity during which we try to be more mindful. Good choices are having a shower, cleaning our teeth, getting dressed, eating breakfast, washing the dishes, walking to the bus stop, or taking out the rubbish. We all do things every day that, unless we are ill or exhausted, don't demand much mental effort. They are the sort of thing we easily do on automatic pilot. One moment we are getting out of bed, wishing it was the weekend, not Monday morning; and the next moment, we are sitting on the bus stuck in traffic and anxious in case we are late for work. And between the two, there is just a blur.

Suppose we choose having a shower as our informal practice. As we stand in the shower, we can notice the sensations of the water hitting and running down our skin, the temperature of the water and the air, and the fragrance of the soap or gel and its texture in our hands. We can feel the contact of our feet on the floor and notice the overall sense of our body: tired, energized, or aching. When our mind wanders off, we just notice that and come back to the body sensations.

The beauty of informal practices is that we get extra mindfulness practice at no extra cost in time. We were going to be standing at the photocopier or the bus stop anyway or to be waiting for our computer to boot up. All we have to do is to remember to be mindful – remembering isn't always easy but, with a bit of practice and effort, we soon learn to do it. It won't be the same as a dedicated, formal practice; but even if all we have time for or remember to do is to take a few breaths with awareness or to feel our feet on the ground and check what our shoulders are doing (good for when we are sitting at a computer), it will make a difference. With our eyes open to the possibilities, we may find all sorts of little gaps opening up during the day that are opportunities to be mindful.

Sometimes people object that some of these gaps, for example the shower, is the space they use to plan the day. If that is a deliberate choice and is actually what you are doing, it could be a good use of the space. We do need time to plan, but planning can easily turn into fretting or overplanning – obsessively going over the same fine details again and again or worrying about outcomes that cannot be controlled. Even if that is when you plan, you could, as an experiment, try a few days of just being mindful in the shower and see what happens. Does your life really fall into chaos (through lack of planning)? Assuming you remember to be mindful when you are in the shower, what is that like and how does that affect your day?

Informal and formal practices mutually reinforce each other. If we have a regular daily formal practice, we are more likely to be mindful at other times of the day. And if we take care in our informal practice of mindfulness in routine activities, we shall find it easier to settle into and to profit from our sitting meditation.

 ## Bonus meditation: Mindful walking (minimum five minutes)

Of all the informal mindfulness practices, mindful walking is perhaps the most immediately pleasurable. It's our recommendation for an informal practice for this week (but feel free to do something else mindfully). There are many ways to approach mindful walking, and here we give a few suggestions.

- Choose a walk of between five and fifteen minutes that you do most days, for example the walk to public transport or to the local shops. If you have a regular walk that lasts longer than fifteen minutes, you could choose to be mindful for just a part of it.
- Alternatively, if you have time, pick a short walk that you could do each day, perhaps round a local park.
- Whatever the walk, go over it in your mind's eye. What are the main landmarks on your walk? You could even draw it – as a simple picture or diagram. This will help you to remember to be mindful when you next do the walk.
- When you are walking, pay particular attention to the feel of your feet on the ground and your breathing. If you find it tricky to do both, start with one or the other. You may find (if your route is not too busy) that you can harmonize your walking with your breathing. You don't need to walk slower than you would normally but you could do that if you wish.
- Whenever your mind wanders off, as in sitting meditation, notice where it has gone to, then come back to your feet or your breath.
- Once you have got used to paying attention to your feet and your breathing, you can try being mindful of other aspects of your experience. You could notice other parts of your body, such as the movement of your legs or the swing of your arms. You could notice the sun, rain, or wind on your face or other exposed parts of your body. Try noticing your emotions and your thoughts (although watch out for just getting caught up in your thinking).

- You can also notice the world around you. Try paying attention to the shapes and the colours. How is the light playing on the buildings or trees? Is there anything new or different that you haven't noticed before? What is the sky like (good to do in a country like the UK where the weather changes so much)? It can be enlivening to tune in to the time of day and season and notice the changes. It can bring you into your life, right now, as it is happening.

We have described mindful walking, in which you are going from one place to another (such as from home to the post office) or making a round trip (for example, around the park), but another approach to mindful walking is when you walk to and fro between ten and twenty paces. This is often done at a much slower pace so that you can really pay attention to the subtle movements of the body and watch the mind more closely. Choose a flat piece of ground where you can walk a few metres, turn and walk back, then turn again, and so on. You might start at a normal pace then slow down as you settle into walking. This can be lovely to do outside in nature, such as a park or garden, but it can also be done inside if you have a long enough stretch to walk to and fro. If you are meditating more frequently (as on a retreat), periods of sitting meditation may be alternated with walking meditation. When done this way, walking meditation becomes more like a formal practice.

Setting up a daily meditation practice

One of the things many people new to meditation struggle with is setting up a daily practice. Often they start a meditation course such as KBT with good intentions, but then they find that somehow sitting meditation at home doesn't happen. Broadly speaking, there are two aspects to consider: practicalities and attitude.

Pick a regular time

Let's take the practicalities first. Deciding on a regular time to meditate makes it much more likely that we shall do it. If each day we have to choose when to meditate, that creates extra mental effort and meditation is more likely to be put off. It becomes easier when it is part of your daily routine like taking a shower or brushing your teeth.

People often ask if there is a best time of day to meditate. The best time is the one when you are most likely to do it. For many people, this can be first thing in the morning. (Once the day has got going, all its activities can take over and the intention to meditate evaporates.) That might mean getting up earlier or it might mean rearranging your morning routine to make time for it. Meditation in the morning can be a good way to set you up for the day, like getting out of bed on the right side. But for some people, mornings are a no-go area. In that case, it might be better to meditate when you get back from work or last thing at night before sleeping.

Meditation in the evening can be a good way to settle the mind after a full day and can make it easier to get to sleep. But the danger is that you get to sleep too quickly, so that there is no real meditation, just being unconscious. In general, if you are a morning person and by the evening can be struggling to stay vertical, morning is probably going to be the best time to meditate. On the other hand, if it takes you two double espressos to get going in the morning and in the evening you are hyped up and have difficulty getting yourself to bed, the evening might be a good time for you to meditate. It is worth experimenting and then settling on a time most likely to be best for you.

Prepare your environment and your mind

You will find it easier to meditate if you prepare for it. One aspect of this is reflecting on your meditation outside meditation. If you start to turn your mind towards meditation before you sit down, it is likely to be easier to settle in. Other practicalities include minimizing disturbances, such as turning off your phone and requesting that those you live with leave you undisturbed for the duration. It helps to have a part of a room dedicated to meditation with your own cushion, stool, or chair for sitting. You could decorate it with flowers, photos, incense, and candles if you wish. Lights and smells are not obligatory: the principle is to create an atmosphere that you find conducive to meditation. Putting some effort into making a space for meditation can help to remind you to meditate and get your mind ready for sitting. Occasionally people get the kit in lieu of doing something, so you might have to watch out for buying (or intending to buy) the cushion, statue, candles, incense, and timer instead of actually meditating if you are prone to that form of procrastination.

Find a buddy

Finding a meditation buddy can support your practice. If there is someone you can talk to about your meditation, agree when you are going to meditate or even meditate together – this can make it more likely that you do meditate. Practising kindness is very much about other people, and so it can be a real help to be involved with others who are trying to do the same as you. You might find a buddy through a local meditation class or a virtual group. You will find some websites that have communities in the resources section (Appendix 2). In addition, some meditation apps have communities that you can connect with.

Choose to meditate – or not

Often people say they don't have enough time to meditate (although people with plenty of time can find it just as hard to set up a daily practice). This could be a practical issue, but it is just as likely to be one of attitude. Of course, if you have two full-time jobs, young children, and ageing parents to look after, it is going to be hard. You will need ingenuity to carve out a little time for yourself, and informal practices are going to be important. But from another perspective, we all have the same amount of time. We all have twenty-four hours each day. We then make choices about how we use that time. It can be liberating to realize that each day we are making a choice. They may be very good choices. For instance, having brought children into the world, we are choosing to bring them up as best we can. We may choose to work long hours because we want to pay a mortgage. Likewise, taking time to meditate is a choice.

Probably there will be more things we would like to do with our twenty-four hours than we can fit into a single day. If we decide that all the other things we want to do in a day are more important or desirable than meditation, so be it. It is much better to consciously decide *not* to meditate and to know why than vaguely to allow our unconscious choices to run our life. If we deliberately examine our priorities, we may find that we do have time to meditate or that we could make some changes to our routine to free up some time.

Having done your best to make time for meditation, there is no point in giving yourself a hard time if you don't meditate. It can be hard enough to sit and watch our mind without adding castigation for the days we don't do it. Telling ourself off will just make meditation a more aversive experience.

Be curious about not meditating

If we don't meditate on a day when we had planned to, it is better to be curious about what happened. We can use not meditating as an opportunity to learn about how our mind works. Our reasons for not meditating, possibly not fully formed, may relate to long-standing patterns. Perhaps we feel we don't deserve to give ourself time to attend to our own mind or maybe we doubt whether we are capable of meditation. We might worry about what other people will think of us if they know we meditate. Alternatively, we might doubt whether meditation will be of any benefit or we may have experienced some discomfort while meditating and this has put us off.

As the views that stop us from meditating are often only partly conscious at best, it is worthwhile spending a little time reflecting, to bring our beliefs into the full light of awareness. We then have a chance to address them. If they relate to old views of ourself that we no longer subscribe to, we have an opportunity to let them go. If we discover that we are unclear about some aspect of meditation or about how to work with, for example, some discomfort we are experiencing, then bringing it to light gives us a chance to try to find out more and to clarify our understanding.

 Written task: Preparing your space for meditation (three minutes)

Spend a few minutes imagining the most helpful space in which you can meditate. Think about the light, space, smell and about how you can make it more attractive. Who will you need to tell about when and where you will be meditating? What time of day will be best, and can you make a commitment to this regularly? How will you minimize disturbances?

Create a list of five small acts you can do straight away that will support your intention to meditate:

1. _____

2. _____

3. _____

4. _____

5. _____

Tips for working in meditation

Savouring

Once we have got used to the basic structure of mindfulness meditation, we can start to notice some of the subtler aspects of our experience. One way of thinking about mindfulness practice is as a repeated coming back into awareness. We pay attention to a body sensation, for example; and, before we know it, the mind is off somewhere worrying or fantasizing. We come to, then return to the body – again and again and again. It can be helpful to really pay attention to that moment of coming to, when we recognize that our mind has been off somewhere. What happens? Is there a subtle (or even not so subtle) irritation at having got caught up again (even though we have been told about it and know that this is what minds do)? Or do we rejoice at being back in awareness? How do we return to the object of attention? Do we rush back to body sensations as though, if we hurry back, no one will notice that our attention has lapsed?

We can experiment with savouring the moment of coming to. We can try really feeling, perhaps luxuriating in, the quality of our mind and body at that moment of awareness. Then, if we tend to rush back, we can try returning to the breath or body in a slow and deliberate way, as though we have all the time in the world.

Checking

Knowing that it is only a matter of time before our mind will wander off, we can develop the habit of checking in with ourself. Every so often during the meditation, we can ask ourself where we are now. We can notice whether we are still fully with the object of the meditation (the breath or the body) or whether some of our attention has slipped away into planning or a daydream. Another approach to this is to look out for tensions in the body. Are we pushing or pulling at something? Even the smallest amount of hankering after an experience, a slight clinging on to something, or a subtle trying to get rid of a thought or feeling will create some physical tension. Maybe just a slight tightening in the jaw or clenching of the hands. With practice, we can learn to recognize these subtle signs and to ease the tension. This will bring us back more fully into the meditation.

Why mindfulness first?

We start by practising mindfulness as a foundation that can help us to cultivate kindness. Let's look at some of the reasons for this.

Getting to know our emotional landscape

If we want to cultivate kindness, or any other emotion or attitude for that matter, we need to know how we are feeling; we need to be mindful of our emotions. It is helpful to know our emotional landscape before we try changing it. Returning to the seed metaphor, we need to know what else is growing, what other seeds lie dormant in the soil of our mind. Is our patch of earth full of tangled brambles and stinging nettles, with seeds of spiky thistles just waiting to sprout? If there is lots of prickly anger, for example, it is better we recognize that. It might mean our first work to develop kindness is learning to be patient with our irritation and finding ways to soothe it. The trouble is – many of us are not very aware of our feelings or have blind spots for particular emotions. Mindfulness can be a way to get to know our habitual emotional responses. We explore more fully how to work with the weeds of the mind in the Chapter 2 (and see Appendix 1 on Kindness meditation: Staying creative if you need more help or run into problems with your meditation).

A key part of our meditation practice may be to name our emotions. They may not always fit into a neat box like sad or angry. It might be more like an icky, grungy heaviness-in-the-belly with a bit of worry feeling or the 'putting the world to rights' emotion. We might personify them like the characters in the film *Inside Out*. In it we find four characters in the head of each person (and animal), personifying four principal emotions: joy, disgust, anger, and sadness. How someone behaves depends on which emotional character is in charge; and sometimes there is conflict, with different emotions trying to wrest hold of the controls. So, for example, we might start to recognize that Ms Righteous Indignation has taken control or that Mr Envious is now holding the reins. Taking a gentle, light-hearted approach to our emotions can also help to create space around them so that we don't get so caught up in them.

Sustaining attention

Mindfulness practice can help us to be more able to sustain attention. True, our mind keeps wandering off, but with practice we may get faster at realizing that we have wandered off and thus be able to have more time with the object of our attention. It is counterproductive to berate ourself when our mind gets caught up in something – apart from being unpleasant, it creates more turbulence. But if we can accept our wandering mind and keep gently returning to the breath or the body, we shall find that over time we have longer periods of staying with the object of meditation. This will assist us in kindness meditations when we are trying to give our attention to ourself or someone else.

Body and breath as helpful tools

A central aspect of mindfulness is learning to become more aware of the body and breath. As we become more familiar with paying attention to the sensations of the body and the movement of the breath, we shall find that they become allies in our practice. We shall discuss using the breath and body sensations more in Chapter 2 when we are practising turning towards difficulties, and we shall carry that into our efforts with kindness meditation. We may use the breath as a vehicle to carry kindness (Chapter 4) and the body sensations, especially in the heart area, as a starting point from which to cultivate kindness.

We can start to see how to balance the effort we make: too much and our mind becomes tense and tight, too little and it is dreamy and distracted. When practising kindness meditation, it is easy to press too hard, making the experience of meditating unpleasant; and so it's useful to be able to recognize this tendency and learn to adjust. During mindfulness meditation, we can also start to recognize how body and mind affect each other. When we feel low, the body is likely to slump; when anxious, it becomes tense. We can use these relationships to change our emotions. If we correct the sagging and sit more upright, our mood may brighten. If we can let go of some of the holding on in our body, our mind may relax a little too. All this brings us more flexibility, giving us a more pliable mind and making it easier when we embark on kindness meditation.

For the sheer pleasure

Mindfulness is about developing a more intimate relationship with each moment of our life. Simple tasks can become highly pleasurable, extraordinarily ordinary if you like. For example, a walk to work, listening to a piece of music, or tasting food will be enhanced when we pay more attention to these everyday experiences. Thus it is not about dismissing ordinary life but vivifying it, making our lives richer in the everyday. As we shall see, when added to kindness, mindfulness becomes the ideal soil in which we can sow the experience of our lives more fully.

To learn about life

Perhaps the most powerful explanation of why mindfulness works is that it helps us to acquire insights about life itself. We start to discover how everything changes, how we create our own suffering so much of the time by resisting change, and how we unconsciously build and rebuild a sense of self.

We discuss mindfulness in the first two weeks of KBT. But just in case there is any doubt, it is not that we need just two weeks of mindfulness and then have to focus only on kindness. Rather, the two mutually support each other. As our practice matures, we are likely to find that we want to practise both mindfulness and kindness and that the qualities of awareness and kindness interweave. To begin with, however, a solid foundation of mindfulness is a real asset.

What mindfulness is not

Not about trying to relax

As we become more aware of ourself, our thoughts, and our feelings, mindfulness can be anything but relaxing. Yet we become less shocked and scared of feelings that arise within us. We become more in tune with and less reactive to our inner experience. We learn to become curious and creatively respond to the emotional weather within us. All this *may* create a degree of relaxation; and if that happens we can enjoy it. But it is not the chief aim of mindfulness. Moreover, like someone tetchily telling us to 'just relax', making relaxation our primary goal is likely to be counterproductive.

Not about emptying the mind of our thoughts

Our mind is always generating thoughts, and our body is always responding with emotions and sensations. When we first start to practise mindfulness, it can come as a bit of a surprise just what a tumble dryer of a mind we have. The internal chatter of our life is something we learn to live with more harmoniously by cultivating a deeper understanding of how our mind works. As we become more mindful, it might feel as though we have fewer thoughts, because we are not fighting them so much.

Not an escape from pain

The paradox of learning to be more mindful is that you will feel better, but only by learning not to escape from pain. Much like a caged animal that, when confined, becomes irascible and tries to escape. When we cultivate mindfulness, we open the cage and create a wide-open field. We make emotional space for pain.

Research box: Health benefits of mindfulness

Over the past fifteen years, the rate of research into mindfulness has increased exponentially. Research shows that a course in mindfulness can change your body and your mind. For example, one study compared an eight-week mindfulness-based stress reduction (MBSR) course with a waiting list control. Then everyone was given a flu jab. Those who had done the MBSR course had a better immune response that those on the waiting list.[2]

The strongest evidence for the benefits of mindfulness pertains to depression and anxiety. However, mindfulness, besides helping with mental health problems, can also improve well-being. Medical students (and probably other health professionals) start their training with high levels of empathy. Unfortunately, as training proceeds, their level of empathy declines. Mindfulness taught to medical students has been shown to boost their empathy.[3] Even if you are not a health professional, enhancing your empathy is useful for interpersonal interactions; and if you get the chance, you might want to select a mindful general practitioner.

Home practice

This week try to spend fifteen to twenty minutes each day practising mindfulness of breath and body and bringing mindful awareness to your regular walk, and record this in Table 1 below.

Table 1: Home practice record for chapter 1

Day / date	Mindfulness of breath and body (circle)	Mindful walking (circle)	Comments
Day 1 Date:	Yes / no	Yes / no	
Day 2 Date:	Yes / no	Yes / no	
Day 3 Date:	Yes / no	Yes / no	
Day 4 Date:	Yes / no	Yes / no	
Day 5 Date:	Yes / no	Yes / no	
Day 6 Date:	Yes / no	Yes / no	
Day 7 Date:	Yes / no	Yes / no	

Record on the practice record form each time you practise, making notes on what happens, including any resistances to doing the practice.

Chapter two

···

What about the weeds?

He who hunts for flowers will find flowers;
and he who loves weeds will find weeds.

Henry Ward Beecher

At a glance

- Suffering is intimately connected to how we use language.
- Experiential avoidance usually makes our suffering worse.
- Acceptance is an antidote to avoidance and can be approached in stages.
- Mindful acceptance differs from self-esteem, whose pursuit can add to our suffering.
- We can practise acceptance in mindfulness meditation by turning towards difficulties.

It is sometimes said that nature abhors a vacuum. If you clear a patch of land, the soil won't stay bare for very long. If you don't plant something else, weeds will soon start to sprout and quickly cover the ground. Seeds are remarkable in that they will germinate only when the external conditions are right; but even with the right conditions in the same batch of seeds, they won't all germinate at the same time. Plants hedge their bets: if the first seeds to germinate are destroyed, more will follow in their wake. Seeds can remain viable for a very long time. The oldest recorded viable seed grown into a plant was a Judean date palm, which was over 2,000 years old and germinated in 2005.

People new to meditation often imagine that practices such as mindfulness will enable them to empty their mind. Coming to meditation fresh with a 'beginner's mind', sometimes we relax into an uncluttered mind-state. But soon the weeds start to appear. Old mental habits quickly reassert themselves. The very practice of mindfulness, like clearing the soil, can seem to make the weeds of our mind sprout more vigorously. Our aim in this course is to sow new seeds, the seeds of kindness, and cultivate a beautiful garden of the mind. But we also need to be able to deal with the weeds – the unhelpful habits of negative self-criticism, ill will, and envy. Just as seeds can endure for a long time before germinating, so the negative habits of our mind can keep appearing. This chapter explores what to do when painful mental states arise.

Suffering, language, and the mind

'Why isn't this working? This is too hard? Maybe I'm not cut out for this sort of activity?'

Does your mind ever say things like this to you? Does your mind drag you into scenarios about the future or warn you about all the possible things that might go wrong? For example, does it ever criticize your efforts or compare you harshly to others? Well, if this all sounds familiar, then we suggest that you, like us, have a normal human mind.

When learning meditation, sooner or later – and it's usually sooner – we run into the habitual mind with all its comparing, judging, and criticizing. Painful emotions such as envy or anger start to arise. Mindfulness allows us to see more clearly what our mind is like, and that doesn't always make us feel comfortable.

So let's take a look at how our mind works, and particularly how we are affected by the use of language. Humans use language in two spheres: public and private. The public includes talking, writing, singing, performing; the private entails thinking, imagining, planning, worrying, and daydreaming. Sometimes the word 'cognition' is used as shorthand for the private use of language.

The mind is not a thing like a stone or a table but an incredibly complex set of interactive mental processes. All these processes of analysing, comparing, remembering, and planning rely on sophisticated systems of symbols that we call human language. The mind is not your friend; nor is it your enemy. It is a double-edged sword: it is useful for many purposes but if we don't use it with care, it will hurt us.

On the plus side, language helps us to predict and plan for the future, to share knowledge, and to learn from the past, but we also use it to lie, to incite prejudice, to criticize, and to compare. Language is both a blessing and a curse. Humans suffer, in part, because we are verbal creatures. Verbal skills have been central to human flourishing and evolution but have also been an unavoidable part of our suffering. So we need to learn to better manage the skills that language has given us.

The typical human approach to solving problems goes something like 'I don't like this. I'll figure out how to get rid of it, and then get rid of it.' In the external world this can indeed be helpful; but when applied to our inner suffering, it often backfires. For example, suppose you have a thought you do not like. For example, 'I shall die one day.' When the thought comes up, we try to stop thinking it. Or if we are struggling, we might have recurring thoughts that cause us pain, such as 'I'm worthless, and no one loves me.'

An extensive literature based on the work of Dan Wegner, a Harvard psychologist, has shown that using suppression to avoid thinking a painful thought works in the short term, but it soon appears more often than before. Thought suppression only makes the situation worse.

If you can, try to isolate a single thought that contributes to your current suffering and put it into a short phrase below.

Don't think about your thoughts (five minutes)

1. Write down a thought that contributes to your suffering.

    _____

2. Approximately how many times have you had the thought in the past week?
3. Now get out your watch and try as hard as you can not to think that thought for the next thirty seconds.
4. Write down the number of times you had the thought, however fleetingly, while you were trying not to think it.
5. Now take another thirty seconds and allow yourself to think anything you want.
6. How many times did you think your thought when you allowed yourself to think anything at all?

As you began to try to suppress your thought, what was your experience? Did it become less distressing, less painful, or more entangled, more painful, more frequent? If your experience was more like the second description than the first, this illustrates that trying to get rid of thoughts is a waste of precious energy.

Experiential avoidance

Language creates suffering, as it leads to what Steve Hayes, the pioneer of ACT (Acceptance and Commitment Therapy), calls 'experiential avoidance'. This is the process of trying to avoid our own experiences (thoughts, feelings, memories, body sensations) even when doing so causes long-term difficulties. For example, because you feel too depressed to get out of bed and don't want to face the day, you stop exercising and lose the benefits that exercise bring you. When we are depressed, the common painful thought 'I'm worthless' is often accompanied by every effort to avoid this thought despite how strongly we believe it. We may try all sorts of addictive or extreme behaviour – alcohol, TV, or excessive sleeping or eating – in vain attempts to numb difficult thoughts. Experiential avoidance leads us to dwell on the past or to fantasize about the future, and in the process to miss out on life in the present.

As shown in Figure 1 below, responding to painful experiences with avoidance causes our suffering to grow. The more we avoid them, the greater the suffering. Something unpleasant happens – an unkind comment from a colleague or a disappointment – that we could call 'natural pain'. When we try to avoid the pain, for example by drinking alcohol, we add to it, perhaps through a hangover or unhelpful behaviour when intoxicated. The more we avoid it the greater the pain.

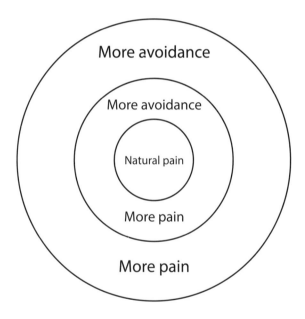

Figure 1: Experiential avoidance causes greater pain

In sum, when we try to run away from a painful thought, body sensation, or emotion, it becomes more important and tends to occur more intensely and frequently. What adds to the confusion is that running away also means we literally become scared, and in turn our thoughts become more believable and entangling.

If we are out of touch with our thoughts and feelings, we lack self-knowledge. Without self-knowledge, it's much harder to change our behaviour. Of course, this is not to insist that people must always be in the here and now. We are all experientially avoidant to some degree some of the time. Nor is it bad or 'pathological'. Rather, avoidance simply stops us from getting the most out of life.

Experiential avoidance is a vicious cycle at the heart of all anxiety disorders and is arguably the single most common factor in all mental health difficulties. We want to encourage people to learn to turn towards their feelings, not just to tolerate them through gritted teeth but to accept them. As research into thought suppression indicates, paradoxically our attempts to reduce our pain often can increase it.

Pain × resistance = suffering

As the adage 'what we resist persists' suggests, when we resist painful experience, we make our suffering worse. Pain means here the unavoidable discomfort of having a body and a mind, such as falling ill or losing someone you love – 'natural pain'. The resistance is our effort to push back and tense up the body or to ruminate in the hope that the pain will go away. It is another form of experiential avoidance.

Suffering is the physical and mental tension created over and above the pain, the bit we have added on by creating further tension.

If we accept that it is impossible to avoid the painful facts of life and that we shall all grow old, get sick, and die, then it seems that the more we add on, the more we obsess, blame, ruminate, and worry, the more intense our pain will become. We suffer when we don't get what we want or lose what we had and when we get what we do not want. The ability to see things as they are, with acceptance, gets us through. As our resistance to pain softens, the less we will suffer.

The same issue applies to our emotions. Most of us, understandably, worry about what could happen if we open up to emotional pain. Depressed people fear that they will be overwhelmed and stuck. Anxious people worry that it will only bring on more intense bouts of anxiety (be that worry, panic, or obsessions). People with trauma in their past might expect that painful memories will surface more often. Those in difficult relationships might fear that if they allow themselves to admit how bad things really are, it will mean that they have to take action.

All these responses are possible. In fact, it is likely that if they are your habitual responses, then probably you will engage in some of them quite naturally. Our intention with this book is to give you some skills to face your pain from a position of confidence and strength.

In short, if you are not willing to feel sadness, for example, and you make every effort to block it out, eventually what you resist persists and grows bigger. One of the first skills we need to learn is how to identify when to face our pain more head on and when to take a more gradual and gentle approach.

What is mindful acceptance?

In the spheres of psychology and therapy, it is increasingly common to encounter ideas of self-acceptance and self-compassion. By this is often meant the importance of learning to turn towards emotional pain rather than to try to fix, remove, or solve it. In previous generations of therapy, when a person came to therapy saying 'life is too much; teach me how to be less stressed', therapists might have been obliging in their efforts to teach relaxation skills.

In a sense, there was an implicit assumption that 'you tell me the issues and we shall solve them together'. What recent research has shown is that what matters is the process of establishing a new relationship with our thoughts and feelings rather than trying to fix them.

This new relationship emphasizes turning towards or accepting emotional pain, using practices of mindfulness and compassion to help us do this. The word 'acceptance' in this context includes a range of experiences from curiosity, tolerance, willingness, and befriending of our emotional pain. Acceptance is not giving in or resigning ourself in a despairing sense. Nor does it mean forcibly resisting our pain or blindly accepting it. So before anything else, we need to be clear about what it is we are accepting.

Stages of acceptance

The process of acceptance does not happen in a linear way: instead, some days we leap forward and other days we drop back. The deeper the pain, or rather the bigger the loss (because all pain is about loss), the longer it takes to pass through these stages.

It is also pointless to try and rush these stages. Pain wants to be processed at its own pace. Trying to rush is like trying to push it away; this only leads to more suffering. So these stages are here as a map for all difficult emotions, to help us navigate with more kindly awareness of what stage we are at. The process is slow and natural and we are really aiming to find a middle way between facing and avoiding our difficulties.

You might feel fragile one day and bullish and confident another day. Given the choice, attempt new challenges only when you are ready, but don't give up either.

Stage one: Aversion

Take the example of the loss of a parent. It can be a life-changing moment of unbearable pain. After a funeral, one's nervous system can be so overrun with emotion that meeting people can feel more like an out-of-body experience, a sense of seeing the world through a glass cage. For instance, seeing someone lose their temper over poor service at a restaurant may feel like witnessing something in a foreign land.

Stage two: Curiosity

At some point, though, a sense of carrying on life as normal is needed. A bargaining between giving up and carrying on in spite of the loss is negotiated. Feeling bad can still seem like a constant experience, but there is enough awareness that you can either succumb to your misery or choose to bring an attitude of curiosity to your painful experience.

Stage three: Tolerance

After a few weeks, perhaps the loss starts to sink in; and although you are not incapacitated with grief, the sense that you are grieving is clear. There is some distance rather than the grief being overwhelming; and as there is also a sense that life is for living, so it is realized that this grief needs to be tolerated.

Stage four: Allowing

The grief might be contained at a safe level by going to visit your parent's grave a few times a year or by occasionally taking out a few of their belongings and looking at them. Psychologically, the loving dimension of the relationship with the parent can be allowed into consciousness without fear that it will disappear. You discover that, when you accept your grief, this is a moment of closeness. You even allow the possibility that having a relationship with the dead person is possible. Grief and gratitude start to entwine as emotions of love for that person.

Stage five: Friendship

At a certain point, allowing oneself to feel grief becomes an act of savouring rather than suffering. It is as though a light bulb gradually gets brighter, and it is now possible to turn towards all the pain of the loss and, in doing so, to find more and more love and friendship.

Mindful acceptance vs self-esteem

In many Western models of psychological well-being, self-esteem is thought to be a good thing, something we should aspire to. The danger with self-esteem is that there is always another, higher standard by which to compare ourself. We might improve our relative standing in the world and be the better for it, but we shall always come up short of another hurdle we need to overcome.

The problem with self-esteem is that it requires social comparison. We might work hard to improve how we feel by finding ways to make ourself feel bigger than others, but there is always someone cleverer, more beautiful, and thinner than us. Mindful acceptance is more empowering than self-esteem because it is something we can do for ourself, without reference to others. We are entering an internal, psychological space for responding actively to our feelings, as we would respond to the texture of our duvet on our skin. We become curious about the direct sensations, as if holding a fragile object in our hands, adopting a gentler, more loving posture towards ourself.

With mindful acceptance, we start to open up to a more emotional life. As if having a spring clean at home, we start to open all the blinds and windows. We begin to let more light in, including into all those dark corners we want no one to see. Mindful acceptance is like turning fresh soil into the earth: it allows those dark, dried-up parts of ourself to be felt. We begin to turn the soil of our mind and to allow the fresh air of life to touch those hidden parts.

As with the growth of a seed, we cannot grow all at once through force and expectation, but only as a result of cultivating patience and trust. With mindful acceptance, we start to bear our emotions with tolerance and curiosity, and eventually we start to give them room, even becoming friends with our more difficult emotions. With patience, we learn to hold more and more of our experience, not having to shame ourself into silence or to avoid our pain with addictions. So even if there is a storm brewing above, we can watch it come and watch it go.

The great storyteller

In KBT, we often talk about thoughts as 'stories'. This is based on the metaphor that our mind is like a great storyteller who constantly gets absorbed and lost in their own story. This master storyteller spins a spellbinding yarn just behind our eyes and crafts the most convincing tales. Like every storyteller, they want our full attention; and they will say anything to get it, even if it's scary and painful. Sometimes the stories are true, and we call them 'facts'. Most of the time, though, they are more like opinions or narratives about how we see the world and what is fair and unfair and what we want to do. Whether or not the story is 'true', our job is to learn to recognize when we have fallen under the spell of a story and to discern whether it is helpful or unhelpful.

For example, we might have a story about getting older and how we shall cope when we are old. Unless we die young, we shall get older and need to face the difficulties that come with that. There will be a time when it is helpful to consider arrangements such as making a will or moving into sheltered accommodation. Getting entangled in a story about ageing and not coping that fills us with fear is likely to feel paralysing and unhelpful. In this case, even though aspects of the story might be 'true', it will usually be more helpful to create some space around it by practising mindful acceptance.

Even our 'positive' stories can be unhelpful if we get too strongly caught up in them or overidentified with them. For example, if we believe that we are a capable person and can master anything, it might give us a helpful can-do attitude to approaching novel tasks. But if we hold on to it rigidly, it might prevent us from getting help when we need assistance or cause frustration because we believe that we should be able to do the new task self-sufficiently.

Mindful acceptance is not itself a single technique but a principle that includes several practices. As a reminder, our aim in these practices is to become more emotionally present and engaged in our experience. The intention is not to feel better or to get rid of unwanted thoughts. Often we find that, as we become more accepting of our emotional state, the painful aspects can seemingly disappear or we can feel better or both. This is merely a bonus, and it won't always happen – so best not to expect it. If we start to use these practices to get rid of unwanted emotions, it can become a control strategy and is ultimately likely to fail. So watch out for this.

A taste of mindful acceptance

We shall now explore a few techniques to get a taste of how this works. It's worth trying the different exercises to see what works best for you. Once you get a sense of what mindful acceptance is like, you can make up your own methods. You can practise this during formal meditation (like mindfulness of breath and body) or informally during the day when you find you get caught by troublesome thoughts. Some of the ways suggested will lend themselves more easily to use in meditation than others, and some may need adapting for use in the moment when you find that your mind gets hooked in daily activities.

Body awareness, in particular, can be a great ally in supporting mindful acceptance. The more we contact the present moment through our body, the more we leave the world of language and stories behind.

 Guided reflection: Feet on the earth (two minutes)

A simple exercise to help centre yourself and connect with the world around you is to ground your feet. This can be especially helpful in moments when we are unexpectedly beset by something distressing.

1. Plant your feet on the floor.
2. Push them down and notice the floor beneath you, supporting you.
3. Notice the muscle tension in your legs as you push your feet down. Notice your entire body and the feeling of gravity flowing down through your head, spine, and legs to your feet.
4. Now look around; notice the sounds around you and notice what you are about to do.

The next exercise helps us to differentiate our emotions more clearly. So often, moment to moment, we find it hard to untangle our inner life; and, when asked how we feel, we have not the faintest idea or we say, 'I'm fine!'

 ## Bonus meditation: Leaves on a stream (five minutes)

1. Find a comfortable posture in a chair or lying down and close your eyes.
2. Imagine you are settling down by a gently running stream and you notice some leaves flowing past on the surface. Imagine this however you like; let your imagination go in whatever direction it wants.
3. For the next minute, place every thought that pops into your mind on a leaf and let it float on by. Try to let the positive as well as the negative thoughts go; let them float past.
4. If your thoughts stop coming, just watch the stream. Sooner or later, another one will pop into your mind and you can carry on placing each on a leaf and letting it float away.
5. Allow the stream to move at its own rate. There is no need to speed it up, to try and blow the leaves away – you are simply letting the thoughts come and go.
6. If a leaf gets stuck by the side of the stream, let it hang around. If a difficult feeling arises such as boredom or impatience, simply acknowledge this too. You could say, 'Here is a feeling of boredom' and place those words on a leaf and let it float on by.
7. When you feel ready, return to sensations of contact with your chair or lying down; become more aware of the sounds around you and open your eyes.

Guided reflection: Labelling your thoughts (five minutes)

A powerful but simple way to disentangle ourself from thoughts that have us under their spell is to label them for what they are.

For example, if you are thinking about things you have to do later today, add a label to the type of thought: 'I am having the thought that I have things to do later.' If you feel anxious, make a note of it by saying to yourself, 'I am having the feeling of anxiety.'

As before, you could start this exercise by allowing your thoughts to float by for a minute as though watching leaves on a stream, paying attention to your body as you do this. Then, as the leaves flow by, you can label them aloud, saying, 'I am having the thought . . .' Saying this aloud can help to create some distance from your thoughts; and, once you get a feel for this, it can be sufficient just to label the thoughts quietly in your mind. When you add your labels, they could take the following forms:

- I am having the thought that . . . (describe your thought)
- I am having the feeling of . . . (describe your feeling)
- I am having the memory of . . . (describe your memory)
- I am feeling the body sensation of . . . (describe nature and location of sensation)

As we start to practise labelling our private experiences, we start to notice a difference between how we relate to the sentences 'I am worthless' and 'I am having the thought that I am worthless'. The latter has more space around it and can become less emotionally charged. We can use labelling during core meditation as well as more informally as we go through our day. Labelling is particularly helpful when we are entangled in a thought or feeling and we are struggling to identify what to do next.

Weeds have nutrients too

Lots of energy is locked up in our negative emotions such as hatred and envy and in our obsessive thoughts. We don't want to lose that energy. Blocking things out doesn't work because it imprisons the energy; it leads instead to a sense of deadness or to being numb. With mindful acceptance, we change our relationship to difficult emotions without losing the energy. It is like pulling up a weed, having a good look at it, and then putting it on a compost heap or back on the ground where it can enrich the soil. Of course more weed seeds will sprout – weeding never ends. But we get better at recognizing weeds when they are still small.

Acceptance is not passivity

Acceptance is more about accepting our private, internal states – thoughts, feelings, and memories – and not passively accepting our life circumstances. Once we do accept what emotions are present, we are in a much better position to decide what to do next. For example, suppose we feel angry after reading an email that we feel is critical of us. We could try to block it out by switching to surfing the internet and shopping for things we don't need or by seeking distraction in pornography. Alternatively we might be incited into sending a curt email back laced with righteous indignation or fall into self-recrimination for our apparent shortcomings. None of these knee-jerk approaches is likely to help in the long run. Mindful acceptance is about recognizing what we feel in the body, but without rushing to fix it.

Often we use terms such as 'expand around it', 'open up and make room for it', 'soften up around it', 'breathe into it', and 'give it some space'. Just in case this isn't clear – accepting does not mean that we think, 'Oh, fantastic. It's wonderful that I feel angry' (whether in a sincere or sarcastic tone). Bringing mindfulness to what is going on is creating a pause, a recognition or acknowledgement of the fact that we are feeling angry. Acceptance points to the atmosphere in which we acknowledge the anger. We are not ticking emotions off like a schoolmistress underlining spelling errors with a red pen.

Instead we try to bring a quality of warmth and friendliness to the painful emotion arising. Part of mindful acceptance may be a recognition that, if we act from our anger, we may cause ourself (and others) more suffering, just as will happen if we get hooked into self-blame. Holding the anger in mindful awareness, we can then decide what to do next, guided by what is important to us. This might include acting with kindness – but more of that from Chapter 3 onwards when we start to focus on cultivating kindness directly.

Another way to think about acceptance is in terms of willingness to have an experience in order to live a fuller, richer life. So every time we encounter a feeling or thought we would rather push away, we can ask ourself, 'Does opening up to this feeling enable me more or less to do what really matters to me?'

Turning towards difficulties

The mindfulness of breath and body core meditation in Chapter 1 is the foundation for practising the second core meditation, mindful acceptance. Our main focus, as described in that chapter, is to pay attention in the first stage to the breath and in the second stage to body sensations more generally. Then, when we find that our mind is ensnared in a difficult experience such as a painful emotion or a physical sensation, or if it keeps getting caught up in the same repetitive or painful thoughts, we can practise mindful acceptance by turning towards the difficult experience and making it the focus of the meditation.

We can do this by noticing just where in the body is being affected, homing in on the particular sensations. Attending to the body in detail can be a good way to shift us out of the unhelpful proliferation of thoughts, such as catastrophizing, that can occur around a painful experience and contribute to perpetuating it. The body gives another place from which to view painful mental experiences. Even if the pain is primarily physical, it is still helpful to move out of the immediate thought reactions to it such as 'I can't bear it' and investigate just what this experience we have labelled 'pain' consists of. At best, we can bring an attitude of allowing and letting be to what is happening, a sense of curiosity and friendliness.

We can use the breath to help us stay with the experience by breathing into the sensations. If they are very intense, we can breathe on the edge of them, softening around the area and holding it gently. Once we have spent some time doing this or it has changed, we can then return to following the breath (in stage one) or the body in general (stage two) as our main focus. When we return to the breath or the body, it is an implicit acknowledgement that the pain is not the whole of our experience. We can also move back and forth, narrowing our attention like a spotlight on to the area of discomfort and then expanding awareness out to include the whole body, as when all the house lights come up in a theatre.

 ## Core meditation 2: Mindful acceptance – turning towards difficulties (fifteen minutes)

Preparation

First of all, we scan through our body. Start by feeling the contact of your feet on the ground. Notice the temperature of your feet and the sensations of any footwear. Gradually move your awareness up your legs. Notice if there is any holding on, especially in the thighs. Allow yourself to feel your body in contact with the clothes you are wearing and in contact with the seat you are sitting on or the surface you are lying on. Become aware of your torso, your back, and your spine. If you are sitting up, feel the natural curves of the spine rising out of the pelvis; and if you are lying down, feel your spine being supported by the ground. Notice any sensations in your neck, your head, and your face. Is there any tightness in the face? If you can, allow the face to soften. Notice your shoulders. Is there any tension there? Take awareness to your arms and hands. If you are sitting up, check that your hands are supported by your lap, so that you can let go of the arms.

Now notice that you are breathing. Feel the chest and perhaps the belly expanding and contracting.

Stage one: The breath

Without trying to change your breath in any way, allow yourself to follow the movements of the breath in and out of the body. Become interested in just what the breath is like: whether it is deep or shallow, long or short, smooth or irregular.

To begin with, when you become aware that your mind has wandered off, just notice where it has gone to and then return gently to the breath. After a while, if you find that you keep getting tangled up in the same experience or if you find that you are having painful feelings, thoughts, or body sensations, choose to turn towards them in an attitude of friendliness and curiosity. See if you can notice just where in the body is affected and what those sensations are like – are they sharp or dull, sustained or changing quickly; do they seem to have a shape or a colour? Use the breath as a probe to explore the sensations or as an anchor to help you to stay present while you turn towards the difficulties. If you find it helpful, you can say to yourself, 'It's OK, whatever it is. It is already here; let me feel it.' Then, when you have spent some time with the difficult experience or you see that it has changed, return to following the breath in and out of the body.

Stage two: The body

Now broaden your awareness to notice any sensations in the body that arise. You might, for example, notice the contact with the ground, the sensation of clothing resting on your skin, one part of the body touching another, or internal sensations. As best you can, be interested in just what the sensations are like. Are they sharp or dull, changing quickly, or more sustained? Just where in the body can you feel them?

Again, if you notice that there is something painful going on or if you keep getting ensnared by repetitive or obsessive thoughts, turn towards the experience, by focusing on the parts of the body that are affected. If it is not obvious which part of the body is affected, for example if you are mainly aware of obsessive thinking, bring your attention to where there are the strongest body sensations or scan through the body to note if there is any tension or holding in parts of the body and attend to those sensations. As best you can, bring a quality of acceptance, allowing, and letting be. Without trying to change the sensations or the experience, explore the qualities of the body sensations. Use the breath to breathe into the sensations or to help you to stay with them. If the sensations seem very strong, you could try allowing the breath to just touch the edges of the area affected and let your attention remain there for a while, softening around the area and holding it gently. Then, when you have spent some time with the experience or it has changed, return to following body sensations in general.

When you are ready, bring the meditation to a close. Pause a little before getting up and then perhaps stretch your body before continuing with your day.

Tips for working in meditation

Trouble-shooting mindful acceptance

1. 'It's not working': When we notice this kind of response to an exercise, it often means that 'I still feel sad or anxious' or that 'I don't like what I am feeling and it ought to go away.' Here we have a control rather than a mindfulness agenda. The overriding impetus is to get rid of painful feelings. Although this is understandable, it backfires. Mindfulness has a quality of willingness to be with whatever arises.

2. 'But it's true': This is often said when we notice we are criticizing a practice because the emotion we are experiencing is true. Our emotions may or may not accurately reflect our life circumstances, for example feeling angry about an insult or poor treatment. Sometimes our emotions might accurately reflect our circumstances, but the issue is not whether they are justified but whether they are helpful. If we hold on to this emotion, does it really help us to act like the person we want to become?

3. Bargaining: This subtle version of control can involve making a deal with a painful emotion, such as 'I'll pay attention to you as long as you clear off in a minute.' Our 'acceptance' is conditional on experiencing a change of emotion, and so is not real acceptance. As long as we hold on to a hope of changing difficult emotions, we are setting ourself up for more suffering. We may only recognize that we have been bargaining when we have tried to be with the experience and then feel disappointed that it hasn't gone away. When we notice bargaining, we can try to let it go or to bring our attention, as best we can with acceptance, to the pain of disappointment that there hasn't been the change we had (perhaps secretly) hoped for.

Home practice

This week try to spend fifteen minutes each day practising mindfulness of breath and body and bringing mindful awareness to your regular walk. As best you can, practise acknowledging and disentangling yourself from unhelpful stories you get caught up in and accepting difficult emotions as they arise, especially by focusing on body awareness.

Record what you did and found on the practice record form (Table 1 below) each time you practise.

Table 1: Home practice record for chapter 2

Day / date	Mindful acceptance meditation (circle)	Mindful walking (circle)	Comments
Day 1 Date:	Yes / no	Yes / no	
Day 2 Date:	Yes / no	Yes / no	
Day 3 Date:	Yes / no	Yes / no	
Day 4 Date:	Yes / no	Yes / no	
Day 5 Date:	Yes / no	Yes / no	
Day 6 Date:	Yes / no	Yes / no	
Day 7 Date:	Yes / no	Yes / no	

Chapter three
Time to sow

No kind action ever stops with itself. One kind action leads to another. Good example is followed. A single act of kindness throws out roots in all directions, and the roots spring up and make new trees.

Amelia Earhart

At a glance

- If we are to cultivate kindness, we need to be clear about what kindness is and is not.
- Hurdles are unhelpful views about kindness that need to be overcome, and masks are 'near enemies' that look like kindness but are not the real thing.
- Authentic kindness includes a feeling of sympathy, thoughts of well-wishing, and an urge to act on those thoughts and feelings.
- The kindness breathing space is a short practice to give kindness to any situation that we find ourself in.
- The basic structure of kindness meditation includes directing kindness towards ourself and to others who elicit feelings of like or dislike or who don't elicit strong feelings either way.
- We can use words and phrases that resonate with us to cultivate kindness in meditation.

In Chapter 2, we started weeding the ground of our mind in order to discourage the presence of some unhelpful habits. Using mindfulness, we started to develop some skills to prevent weeds from growing bigger and taking up valuable space and nutrients in our heart. But sometimes it is quite difficult to tell a flower from a weed. In the first half of this chapter, we shall discuss our views on kindness and learn to differentiate between flowers and weeds. As we have seen, we need to give our seeds the best chance to grow; and by first examining our views on kindness, we are creating the most fertile conditions possible.

Through the practice of mindfulness, we have started to tune in to the subtleties of our physical and emotional life. We have already had to face up to uncomfortable emotions and body sensations and then to begin to allow and bring more acceptance and curiosity to our experience. Now we need to turn our curiosity to what we think kindness actually is. You only have to google the word to be hit with '95,700,000 results (0.54 seconds)' and a dizzying array of images and phrases. But not of all these results will point us to the seeds we hope to sow in this book.

Hurdles and masks

When we first try to generate kindness towards ourself or others, we often come unstuck, although it may not be clear why. And we tend to think, Of course kindness is a good thing. Who would disagree with that? But the biggest hurdle is not the lack of kind people out there but often our own views and attitudes about kindness.

 ## Guided reflection: Meanings of the word kindness (one minute)

Sometimes our views about kindness are not so obvious. Let's get you reflecting on this topic: bring to mind what you associate with the word 'kindness'. You can use the spider diagram opposite to catch any words (positive or negative) that pop into your mind that sum up what kindness means to you.

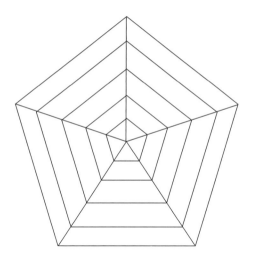

Figure 1: Web of kindness

There are some common misunderstandings of kindness (hurdles) and some 'near enemies' that masquerade as kindness but aren't the real thing (masks). We need to be clear about the difference between authentic and false kindness, for two reasons. Firstly, if what we think is kindness actually is not, it can put us off making an effort to begin with. Secondly, when we are cultivating kindness, we need to be alert to the pitfalls that can lead us away from authentic kindness. Much like weeds that look like flowers, they will take up our precious soil, not serving our garden at all.

Hurdles

Hurdles are assumptions that prevent us from even bothering to sow seeds of kindness in the first place. Often they are mixed up with more helpful views about kindness, but they can be difficult to spot. Below are some common assumptions that can deter us from cultivating kindness.

Kindness is a sign of weakness

Somewhere along the way, almost all of us have picked up the belief that to be kind is the soft or weak option. If you are kind, you don't stand up for yourself or someone else. Contrary to what people tend to believe, cultivating kindness requires facing up to our difficulties and showing a willingness to experience a range of emotions.

Kindness will make me a doormat

Another version of kindness as weakness is the view that being kind means you open yourself up to be 'walked all over' or taken advantage of. Sometimes people believe being kind means that you do not stand up to a situation, including standing up for yourself. For example, someone may put up with a partner's aggression under the guise of being 'kind' to them. There could be many reasons why someone might put up with this behaviour, such as believing they deserve it or for fear of making the aggression worse, but it's not kindness. Indeed, the belief that they deserve it indicates a lack of kindness towards oneself. To be truly kind may mean standing up to difficult situations and so may need much courage.

Kindness will only set me up for a fall

Another common view is that accepting kindness from others leaves you open to upset and disappointment. In other words, accepting kindness from others is the same as 'People are only saying that' or 'If they really knew me, they wouldn't feel that way'. Sometimes people are more generally wary of positive moods, as if they are being set up for a fall. Or perhaps they think feeling good will attract negative things as a sort of payback.

Thanks to our brain's 'better safe than sorry' default setting (discussed in Chapter 4), our threat system often ends up in overdrive running the show. However, cultivating kindness actually fine-tunes your threat system to run more efficiently, helping you to decide when to put your guard up and when not to. Ultimately, applying kindness is about making wiser choices.

Kindness means putting my needs last

For some people, their needs are not as important as others'. This is especially common for individuals who are highly self-critical. When we constantly put the needs of others first, we can subsequently feel resentment if we feel taken for granted, not cared for, or simply exhausted. Authentic kindness starts with learning to recognize that you have needs and cultivating a non-judging attitude towards them. As we shall discover, true kindness does not come from a feeling of lack.

Kindness is manipulative

Conversely, apparent kindness can be disguised as manipulation. This is not to say that we should expect to always have pure, unselfish motivations. Acting with kindness is likely to have all sorts of benefits for us, such as feeling happier and being liked by others, and our awareness of that should not stop us from acting with kindness. At the same time, we can want the best for ourself and the best for others, and kindness can help with both. This is different from deliberate ingratiation, in which we are only in it for what we can get. Usually we can feel the difference. This sort of apparent kindness often doesn't ring true, as if we are being sweetened up so that something can be asked of us.

Kindness takes too long to develop

In this age of consumerism, there can be a belief that our personal wants should and can be gratified not tomorrow, not later today, but now. A bias towards fulfilling our immediate wishes has left us cold to the slow pace of kindness. Being kind is not cool or sexy, nor does it necessarily gratify us immediately. Perhaps this view is most perniciously summed up in our modern cynicism as 'I tried it once before. Why bother being kind again?'

We need to watch out for judging ourself for acting on good intentions that have consequences we did not expect or hope for. Developing kindness is about learning to make better judgements and accepting with a kindly attitude that we won't always get it right or get what we want. Most of all, though, we need to be patient and to accept that the process and evolution of kindness need time to flower.

Kindness means not facing up to difficult emotions

In fact, kindness means experiencing difficult emotions rather than turning away from them. It's about taking responsibility for and validating difficult emotions such as sadness, anger, and anxiety. Only when we have acknowledged difficult emotions and allowed ourself to experience them can we develop the courage and creativity to work with them. Kindness helps to develop the strength to put yourself in challenging situations in order to build the self-confidence to face your fears.

Developing kindness will be too hard or overwhelming

It is not uncommon that when we start to develop kindness, especially towards ourself, we can feel emotions that have been bottled up and that may come flooding out. Understandably, we sometimes fear that strong emotions will overwhelm us and maybe even make us 'mad'. At the very least, we may believe that allowing these emotions to be felt will have a destabilizing effect. In the short term, developing kindness might feel hard or overwhelming, and emotions will undoubtedly come to the surface. But in the long term, it is rewarding to feel the full range of our emotional life.

Masks

Masks are emotions that look superficially like kindness but are not the real thing. Much like a weed with pretty flowers, the beauty is diverting our attention away from the fact that it is a weed. We may sense it is a mask when we get a whiff of such 'kindness' directed towards us and find ourself wanting to back off. What is more likely is that, as we start to practise more kindness, we sometimes slip into wearing a mask. Much like a weed masking itself as a pretty flower – we like the look of it and leave it in the ground. By learning to spot these weeds, we can uproot them before they take hold.

Kindness is sentimental

Sometimes we hear the phrase 'he or she meant well'. For example, your old school friend appears really upset that your relationship ended but they make no effort to help you. Sentimentality is an excess of emotion – all the right noises but they don't translate into helpful action. Conversely, authentic kindness is positive emotion plus action.

Although we may sometimes make mistakes in acting on our good intentions, true kindness is not without good judgement. Merely acting in a blanket 'kind' way that doesn't see the needs of the other person whom we are supposedly being kind towards is not kindness. There is an element of wisdom in authentic kindness.

Kindness is pity

Pity takes a position of superiority: 'Oh, poor you!' It acts to keep us at a distance from someone's troubles, as to get any closer might be threatening. Self-pity is similarly a way of not really facing up to what is going on, by holding on to a distressing emotion.

 ## Weeding exercises (five minutes)

Remember that we are all likely to have developed a mixture of hurdles and masks. Now is a chance to untangle these weeds and to uproot a few for closer examination. This entails simply bringing these views into more awareness. Go back over the ones described above and tick those that apply to you. In particular, see if you can identify your top three – either the hurdles or the masks that you are going to be on the lookout for.

Identify pros and cons of accepting kindness from others and developing kindness towards yourself (five minutes)

Another way to identify weeds is to reflect on the pros and cons of developing kindness. In the table below, we give some of the common pros and cons, in terms of both cultivating kindness towards ourself and giving and receiving kindness from others.

Table 1: Kindness: Pros and cons

Cons of accepting kindness from others	Pros of accepting kindness from others
I'll only open myself up to be disappointed later. I shall have to give something back in return.	I might get the warm glow of feeling supported and liked by others. It could help me feel closer to others.
Cons of developing kindness towards myself	**Pros of developing kindness towards myself**
I shall drop my guard and become more naïve and less able to solve problems. I shall become lazy and weak and get nothing done.	I might start to feel more self-confident. I might accept my shortcomings and stop attacking myself when things don't go my way. Life might feel a bit easier and less stressful.
Cons of developing kindness towards others	**Pros of developing kindness towards others**
People will take advantage of me. I shall get nothing in return.	I shall strengthen my relationships with others. I shall feel good about myself for being generous.

Now fill in the boxes in the table below with your own pros and cons.

Table 2: Kindness: My pros and cons

Cons of accepting kindness from others	Pros of accepting kindness from others
Cons of developing kindness towards myself	Pros of developing kindness towards myself
Cons of developing kindness towards others	Pros of developing kindness towards others

Written task (two minutes)

Reflecting on the pros and cons of cultivating kindness, do you notice any patterns? Is any box overloaded with strong views? What are your most obvious hurdles? Take a moment to list any useful reminders – things you can do or say to yourself to help you with the cons.

- _____

- _____

- _____

- _____

 Guided reflection: Working with views in meditation (three minutes)

When we are practising kindness meditation, it is worthwhile to watch out for unhelpful views popping up. Sometimes these views stop us from really making an effort to try something out. You can do this exercise in a few minutes to help.

First bring your attention to your breath. As you breathe, notice any thoughts or judgements running through your mind about 'Why am I bothering to do this right now?' Just spend a minute noticing any masks or hurdles to kindness as they arise.

Then, as you notice a hurdle, gently introduce a word such as 'acceptance' or 'allow', as if you were dropping a pebble into a still pool. Then wait for any ripples, however faint.

You might say the word quietly to yourself and then sit with awareness of any body sensations, feelings, emotions, or thoughts that arise. If your mind wanders, just bring your attention back to any body sensations. It can be helpful to give attention to the heart area or the belly.

Conclusions

Bear in mind that these masks and hurdles are very common. Just because you notice them in your mind does not mean that they are uniquely yours or, indeed, factually true. Hurdles can be jumped with growing ease and fluidity, but the first job is to acknowledge them. Consciously, and mostly unconsciously, we have allowed them to be there or have put them in place, often for good reason – usually to keep us safe. In short, the hurdles or basic views of kindness have served a purpose, most likely to protect us, and now we are trying to update them.

These hurdles and masks are the weeds. They will have grown in response to your environment, relationships, and upbringing. Learning to deal with them afresh will require you to approach them with respect for how long they have been around. Some weeds will be relatively easy to pull out by simply becoming more aware of them. Others, deep-rooted, like bindweed, have been present for many years and will require more effort, more of a leap of faith and patient persistence.

We would encourage an attitude of approaching this book as an experiment, trying to be as open and objective as possible to test your predictions by gathering new evidence. As with all things worth investing in, there are no quick fixes. But, with the exercises that follow, you will start to negotiate these hurdles with more confidence.

You can also practise noticing hurdles and masks as you are walking to work or are in the middle of doing something. As you do, try to cultivate an attitude of mindful acceptance towards these weeds. Chances are that some have been around for a long time; and, although it would be nice to uproot them in one go, they might keep popping back up. Our job is simply to not let them dominate the garden of our mind and stop us from making an effort to sow of seeds of kindness.

Authentic kindness

We have devoted a good bit of this chapter to recognizing masks and hurdles. Clearing up these misunderstandings can help us to bring authentic kindness into sharper focus. Let's begin with some dictionary definitions of kindness, to help us contextualize our understanding of this word. The *Oxford English Dictionary* states that kindness is 'the quality of being friendly, generous, and considerate'. The origins of the word 'kind' go back to before the year 900 AD, and it is one of the oldest words in the

English language. It is derived from the Old English *gecynde*, meaning natural, native, innate, and originally from the word for family. Our word 'kin' comes from it. This suggests that kindness is a natural state, the way that one might naturally be predisposed to one's family (tensions and conflicts that occur in families notwithstanding).

Turning to the Latin, we find that quite a few words were used to mean kindness, each with a slightly different shade of meaning. Looking at some of these can help to fill out various connotations of kindness. Here we have summarized four Latin meanings of kindness, to give a flavour of the breadth of meaning of the word.

1. *Gratia*: favour, goodwill, friendship, grace, gratitude.
2. *Candor*: goodness, integrity, moral excellence, tenderness, benevolence.
3. *Beneficium*: beauty, heat, glow, radiance, purity.
4. *Benevolentia*: courtesy, nobleness, frankness, generosity, gift.

No one meaning encapsulates the term; there are many shades of meaning. In our effort to distil this breadth of meaning, we regard kindness as including the following dimensions: motivation/intention; feeling/sensory; and impulse/behaviour.

The motivation aspect of kindness includes a friendly, helpful, cooperative attitude towards ourself and others. This suggests a motivation based on genuine care for our and others' well-being. Motivation suggests a desire. It is the volitional part of us that might not feel 'nice and kind'. But, as a starting point, there is an intention to be helpful, friendly, and full of goodwill.

The feeling aspect is a sense of sympathy, a feeling for the subject of our kindness (us or others). We might experience this as a sense of warmth, perhaps a glow in the heart. For some people, this can be a strong component of kindness; for others, it may be hardly discernible. It is likely to vary over time as well.

The impulse element of kindness is the urge to act with kindness. Kindness naturally expresses itself in action. However, we may need courage to act with kindness or may need to overcome forces of habit or inertia. To really be kind means to see what is going on and how to respond appropriately and generously. Thus authentic kindness includes an element of grace and wisdom. The more we practise acting with kindness, the wiser and more skilfully we are able to respond.

In sum, we define kindness as the motivation for the well-being of oneself and other people, coupled with a willingness to act on that desire.

Kindness in context

The biopsychosocial model of health and illness is a framework developed by George Engel in 1977.[1] It states that interactions between biological, psychological, and social factors determine the cause, manifestation, and outcome of wellness and disease. According to the biopsychosocial model, interactions between people's genetic make-up (biology), mental health and personality (psychology), and sociocultural environment (social world) contribute to their experience of health or illness. The biological influences on mental health and mental illness are varied, and include genetics, infections, physical trauma, nutrition, hormones, and toxins. The psychological component looks for potential psychological explanations for a health problem, such as lack of self-control, emotional turmoil, or negative styles of thinking. Social and cultural factors are conceptualized as a particular set of stressful events (being made redundant, for example) or supportive influences (such as having a good network of friends) that can differentially affect mental health depending on the individual and their social context. The biopsychosocial theory posits that each one of these factors is not sufficient to create health or mental illness but that the interaction among them determines the course of our development.

The reason for mentioning this model here is to highlight that kindness does not arise in a vacuum. Health promotion, most broadly, must address all three factors. As a growing body of empirical literature suggests, the combination of health status, perceptions of health, and sociocultural barriers to accessing health care influence the likelihood of a patient engaging in health-promoting behaviour, such as taking medication, following a proper diet or nutrition, and participating in physical activity. Just the same, it is the combination of biological, psychological, and social factors that will determine our engagement with the practices suggested in this book. Although it focuses especially on the psychological components, we recognize that biological and broader social processes are impinging all the time on our capacity to promote well-being.

 ## Bonus meditation: Kindness breathing space (three minutes)

The kindness breathing space is a short practice to help us pause, notice what is happening, and bring a sense of kindness to whatever situation we find ourself in. It is a great complement to the core meditation. In our busy lives, we can easily go from activity to activity without recognizing how we are feeling or even what we are doing. We may then act in ways we regret or miss opportunities to respond to situations more creatively. The three-minute breathing space has three steps, AGE:

1. **Awareness** of body sensations, feelings, and thoughts. Check in with yourself, noticing body sensations, thoughts, and emotions.
2. **Gather** the breath, connect with your breathing. Follow the sensations of breathing without trying to do anything to the breath.
3. **Expand** the breath throughout the whole body. Extend kindness to yourself and everyone around you, for example saying to yourself, 'May we all be free from suffering.'

Good times to practise the kindness breathing space are when you are a bit bored or irritated, for example queuing at the supermarket, stuck in a traffic jam, or sitting on the tube or bus. We can do it while we wait for the photocopier or for our computer to boot up. The breathing space acts as a reminder for us to pause and reflect on what is going on in the mind in the midst of our daily life. This practice is a cornerstone of KBT, a go-to short practice that can be used at any time, and something we shall return to throughout this book.

Guided reflection: Attending to body sensations with and without kindly awareness (ten minutes)

As we explored in Chapter 2, pain is inevitable, but how we respond when something painful happens is the difference between creating more or less suffering. The next practice is a slightly longer exercise than the breathing space and takes around five minutes. It helps us to notice the difference between giving attention to our body sensations with and without kindness. Don't worry if you can't feel a difference – this is just one way to begin to practise kindness in meditation.

Establish yourself in a relaxed, upright posture (or, if you prefer, do this lying down). For a couple of minutes, scan the body noticing sensations. Try to do this in a neutral way, perhaps as storekeeper making an inventory of stock; just notice what is there, the pleasant, unpleasant, and neutral areas of sensation.

Now scan the body again for several more minutes, trying to bring a friendly or kindly attention to your different body sensations. As you notice each sensation or body area, imagine greeting each one in a friendly way, like greeting guests at a party. Take your time to just notice what effect the greeting has on this area of sensation. Bring the exercise to a close when you are ready.

What were the differences between the two ways of approaching the exercise? In particular, what differences could you feel in the body with each approach?

Mindfulness of emotions and the body

However you found the last exercise, at the very least you were practising the core skill of becoming more aware of direct sensations in the body. We want to emphasize that emotions always have a component in the body and are best addressed there.

Sometimes, emotions seem to get stronger and stronger the more we fight them, without our noticing a cascade of internal events that has unfolded just beyond the field of our awareness. A common sequence in someone who gets anxious is:

'My heart is racing.'
'I don't like this sensation.'
'I should not have this feeling.'

'I must be seriously unwell if I am feeling this.'
'I can't cope' or 'I'm going to die.'

The earlier we can intervene and notice what is happening in the body and respond with kindness, the better chance we have of interrupting this downward spiral into full-blown panic. This is not easy to do in the moment, and so we need to practise anchoring our emotions in the body. By identifying the body component of a difficult emotion, for example butterflies in the stomach, tightness in the throat, or clenching in the thighs, we are more likely to catch early on the mental suffering that is likely to follow. The key to this next exercise is an attitude of friendliness when we encounter emotions in the body, be they pleasant, unpleasant, or neutral.

 ## Bonus meditation: Kindly awareness of body sensations (five minutes)

In this exercise, which should take around five minutes, we aim to notice pleasant, unpleasant, and neutral body sensations in turn. We try to bring a friendly curiosity to whatever sensations we find in our body.

Begin by establishing a relaxed, upright posture (or by lying down if you prefer). Notice that you are breathing and allow your attention to settle on the breath for a few in-breaths and out-breaths. When you are ready, notice any pleasant sensations in the body. They might not be very strong, perhaps just a sense of ease or a slight relaxation in some part of the body or a sensation of warmth. As best you can, bring kindly attention to these sensations, a friendly curiosity to whatever is there. Allow yourself to enjoy the pleasant sensations.

Now notice any unpleasant sensations in the body. There may be some aches or pains, some tension or restlessness. Just as you did with the pleasant sensations, bring as best you can a kindly awareness to the unpleasant sensations. If you find it helpful, use your breathing to help explore the sensations, feeling into them with a sense of friendliness and curiosity. Try to notice just what the sensations are like and exactly where in the body you are feeling them. Is there an image, a colour, or a shape for these sensations? Allow whatever is there with a kindly interest.

Now notice any neutral sensations, any sensations that do not register as being either pleasant or unpleasant. Again, bring a friendly awareness to them as best you can. Try to feel just what they are like, whether they are strong or weak, whether they change or seem to be still. At any time, if your mind wanders off or struggles to engage with the sensations, just note that this is happening and gently bring your awareness back to the body sensations.

Finally, allow yourself to notice whatever body sensations appear to you, whether they are pleasant, unpleasant, or neutral. As best you can, bring a friendly curiosity to whatever arises, a sense of holding the sensations in kindly awareness. When you are ready, gently bring the meditation to a close.

In summary, we are looking to develop a soft, loving attitude towards the body. We are learning to tune in to that instinctive tendency to tense up and avoid discomfort in the body. As we hold in mind the stages of acceptance mentioned in Chapter 2, befriending unpleasant body sensations can sometimes feel a step too much. So bring an attitude of kindness to this feeling of it being too much as well. We are allowing the body to release and soften as much as seems possible for today. In this way, we are learning not to rush our expectations about 'getting it right', thereby embodying the same message we are giving to our body. For now, we are tuning into our intention to be kinder to ourself; and as with every meditation practice in the book, it starts in the body.

This brings us to our first formal kindness meditation of the book. Each meditation uses different tools to sow the seeds of kindness. Much as gardeners have their preferred tools, we need to discover ours. This chapter introduces our first tool in meditation: words and phrases of kindness. Before this, we shall introduce the basic structure of the meditation that is used in every subsequent meditation.

Kindness meditation: The basic structure

Throughout the book, we shall be following the same structure for the kindness meditation. There are five stages: us, a friend, a neutral person, a person we find difficult, and then all beings. In KBT we are aiming to cultivate kindness towards ourself and towards other people. In the meditation, we start with ourself.

It is good to start here, to tune in to ourself, as a foundation to cultivating kindness. This stage is also one that many people struggle with. To help, we shall include tips for working with this stage at various points in the book. It is also worth remembering that just to give attention to ourself, to notice what is happening in our body, thoughts, and feelings, is itself an act of kindness. Sometimes just that attention is enough.

Like the short body exercises in this chapter, the next three stages cover the different possible 'feeling-tone' responses to people: we like them, dislike them, or are indifferent. Sometimes we may have mixed feelings or our feelings towards someone may change over time. In these three stages we are building resilience, in that we are learning to develop a response of kindness regardless of our immediate reaction of like or dislike of people.

Generally we shall have positive feelings towards a friend. For this stage, especially when we are learning kindness meditation, we recommend picking someone with whom we have a relatively uncomplicated relationship. This will make it easier to cultivate authentic kindness, as opposed to a mask. So we suggest picking someone who is alive (to avoid the complication of grief responses), roughly the same age (to avoid relationships coloured by parent-child dynamics), and to whom we are not sexually attracted (as these relationships often bring many other emotions with them). Hopefully you can find a friend within these categories! As you become more experienced in cultivating kindness, you may wish to extend the range of people whom you include in this category of friend.

For the neutral person, we suggest you pick someone for whom you do not have strong feelings of like or dislike. Within seconds of coming across someone, we make an appraisal of them, including whether we like or dislike them. It is rare that someone we have met evokes no response of like or dislike, even if it is only a mild response. We suggest that you choose a person whom you actually know, at least a little bit, rather than an imagined person or someone you have heard of but never met. In this stage, we are working to cultivate kindness where there is little liking or disliking. The challenge in this stage is to stay interested. We may need to use our imagination more fully to see them as another human being, with thoughts, feelings, and plans just like us. For this stage, you could pick a colleague at work whom you don't have much association with or a local shopkeeper from whom you buy your milk or bread but otherwise don't know well.

The fourth stage is someone we don't like, which generally we shall abbreviate and refer to as 'the difficult person'. 'The difficult person' is not necessarily objectively difficult (just as the neutral person in their own eyes or their friends' eyes is unlikely to be neutral), but this is someone whom we struggle with in some way. We can select someone we generally tend to dislike or with whom we have recently had a disagreement, or someone who does not like us. If there is someone you have strong feelings of ill will towards, perhaps someone who has caused you significant hurt, we recommend that you don't start with them. Instead of cultivating kindness, you could end up developing its opposite! So why include this stage, particularly if there are people in your life who have harmed you in some way?

To be clear, we are cultivating kindness, not liking. So we are not trying to like everyone or, worse, to pretend that we like everyone. Cultivating kindness does not mean approving of everything that someone does, including those actions we don't like or behaviour that we would never wish to emulate. Nor does it mean forgetting the cruel or unkind actions of others or laying ourself open to future similar behaviour. For our own sake, cultivating kindness towards the difficult person is beneficial because holding on to ill will is painful. Nursing resentment poisons our heart.

It is also likely to be beneficial to others, even apart from the difficult person, as hatred and resentment tend to leak out or to find expression in other relationships. When discussing this stage (and the following stage in which we cultivate kindness towards all beings), often people bring up extreme examples such as Hitler or Stalin or less extreme but still contentious examples such as perpetrators of child sexual abuse. We would advocate treating even the difficult person themself with kindness as another human being, in order to foster the sort of world where all are treated as people.

For some, this may feel like a step too far; but, for our own sake, we may still wish to cultivate kindness towards very difficult people. When reflecting on this stage, we may need to remind ourselves that cultivating kindness does not mean being weak or becoming a doormat. Thus, for this stage, we recommend that you start with people towards whom there is only a bit of ill will. Stick to people you know personally and, as you become more confident with the practice, gradually work up to people towards whom you have stronger or more complicated reactions.

In the final stage, we are aiming to cultivate an equality of kindness. That is, we are trying to develop an open-heartedness so that anyone we come into contact with is met with kindness. We begin this stage by including everyone from the first four stages: us, the friend, the neutral person, and the difficult person. We aim to cultivate a quality of kindness equally towards each person – as if we had a wonderful gift and would be equally happy to give it to any of the four people. This is a high aspiration, so we should not be down on ourself if we don't quite feel like this. Rather, we can hold it lightly as an intention and trust that this alone will have a beneficial effect on our heart.

We then expand our kindness outwards as widely as our imagination will allow us, in principle to all beings. We can do this by imagining different geographical regions, perhaps spreading out from where we are. Or we could imagine different types of people, such as all people who are ill, all people who are unemployed, all people whose birthday is today, and so on. Or we could simply bring kindness to whoever comes to mind. For this stage, we shall include people we don't personally know. We can imagine our kindness shining on everyone, like the sun shining in all directions.

One final tip before we get started: it is worth choosing who you are going to put into stages two, three, and four before you start the meditation. This can help to prevent spending time during the meditation deliberating on or switching between people. We suggest that you use just one person per stage until the final stage. If someone else comes to mind, you can always include them in a subsequent meditation.

Core meditation 3: Kindness meditation using words and phrases (twenty minutes)

In this meditation, we use words or phrases associated with kindness. Pick three or four that resonate with you and stick to them for the period of meditation. You could select words you wrote on the spider diagram that have a positive association for you. You can always try other ones at other times, and you may well find that what resonates with you changes over time. Some examples include 'May I be happy', 'May I be well', 'May I be free from suffering', 'May I be at peace', 'May I be safe', and 'May I live with ease'. Or just use a word such as 'happy', 'well', 'safe', 'calm', or 'peace'.

Preparation

As in Chapter 2, before you begin to meditate, try to spend a few minutes preparing for meditation. You might like to light a candle or some incense. If you have time, you could tidy your room a little or have a cup of tea and sit quietly.

Once you are ready, settle yourself onto your cushion or chair. Remind yourself which words or phrases you are going to use and decide which people you are going to put into the meditation. Then bring awareness to sensations in your body, especially the contact with the ground and the chair or cushion. Take time to notice what is going on in the body and, as best you can, allow the body to settle like a sheet coming to rest on the ground.

Stage one: Self

Now say to yourself (silently) one of the phrases or words that you have chosen. As best you can, let the tone of your internal voice be friendly, gentle, and caring. Pause after saying the phrase or word to notice what the effect is. Don't worry if there doesn't seem to be much of an effect. Just sit with awareness of the body and, if you wish, the breath. Then repeat another word or phrase. If you want to, you can use the same phrase or word again. Continue in this way, saying a word or phrase and then allowing a space just to be with whatever arises.

Stage two: Friend

Bring to mind a friend. Notice what the effect is of bringing a friend to mind. You might notice sensations in the heart area or become aware of feelings or emotions. Then say one of your words or phrases, directed towards your friend, for example: 'May X (your friend) be happy.' Continue as in stage one, alternating between a word or phrase and sitting with whatever happens. You could also include yourself, for example: 'May X and I be happy.'

Stage three: Neutral person

Bring to mind a neutral person. Notice what the effect is of bringing this person to mind. Then say one of your words or phrases directed towards the neutral person, for example: 'May X (the neutral person) be free from suffering' or 'May X and I be free from suffering'. Continue as in stage one, alternating between a word or phrase and sitting with whatever happens.

Stage four: Difficult person

Bring to mind someone you don't like or are in conflict with. Notice what the effect is of bringing this person to mind. Then say one of your words or phrases directed towards the person you find difficult, for example: 'May X (the difficult person) be at peace' or 'May X and I be at peace'. Continue as in stage one, alternating between a word or phrase and sitting with whatever happens.

If you find that you are getting overwhelmed with strong negative emotions such as feeling ill will towards the person, then direct the word or phrases towards yourself as in stage one. Try to bring an attitude of kindness towards yourself as you struggle with difficult emotions. Then, when you feel able, return to the difficult person.

Stage five: All four people and all beings

Now bring to mind all four people: yourself, a friend, the neutral person, and the person you find difficult. Repeat the word or phrase for all four of you, for example: 'May we all be happy.' Sit as best you can with whatever arises.

Gradually expand your awareness to include all beings – as far as your imagination will take you, saying 'May all beings be happy'. Continue to alternate between a phrase or word and just sit with whatever arises.

Concluding the meditation

Let go of all beings and come back to yourself. As best you can, let go of all effort. Just sit quietly, simply breathing for a couple of minutes before bringing the meditation to an end.

Tips for working in meditation

Lowering expectations

When we first learn to practise kindness meditation, we can come unstuck owing to our expectations of what should happen, especially in the first stage. We might be expecting to have strong feelings of kindness towards ourself but then feel despondent when perhaps we don't have strong, warm feelings and also become aware of negative, critical thoughts towards ourself. The first thing to do is just to acknowledge what is happening. Giving ourself attention in this way, as we did when practising mindfulness in the first two weeks, is itself an act of kindness towards ourself. The intention for kindness is the most important aspect. We may or may not have strong feelings, and in any case they tend to wax and wane. Instead of worrying about how we feel towards ourself, we can keep returning to an intention, a desire to wish ourself well. Our well-wishing may simply involve bringing as kindly an attitude as we can muster to whatever arises, including thoughts or feelings of ill will directed at ourself or at someone else.

Home practice

This week, try to spend fifteen to twenty minutes each day practising the kindness meditation using words and phrases. Also, see if you can practise the kindness breathing space three times per day – perhaps in the morning, afternoon, and evening.

Record on the practice record form in Table 3 below (and in later chapters) each time you practise, circling a K each time you do a kindness breathing space. Also, make a note of anything that comes up in the practice, especially any masks or hurdles that you notice, to help you reflect on the practice.

Table 3: Home practice record for chapter 3

Day / date	Kindness meditation with words (circle)	Kindness breathing space (circle)	Comments
Day 1 Date:	Yes / no	K K K K	
Day 2 Date:	Yes / no	K K K K	
Day 3 Date:	Yes / no	K K K K	
Day 4 Date:	Yes / no	K K K K	
Day 5 Date:	Yes / no	K K K K	
Day 6 Date:	Yes / no	K K K K	
Day 7 Date:	Yes / no	K K K K	

Chapter four

Waiting for the first shoots

Whenever I feel blue, I start breathing again.
L. Frank Baum

At a glance

- The three emotion-regulation systems – threat, drive and soothing system – can help us to understand how our emotions work.
- The breath and the organ of the heart are intimately connected through the vagus nerve.
- The breath then can help with being mindful of our emotions and cultivating kindness.
- We can use the kindness breathing space as a springboard for taking kindly action.

Kindness is hardwired

From a meditation journal: 'I knew that the meditation wasn't going well when I came to, mechanically repeating to myself "May I be well, may I be happy." I wasn't even trying to do a kindness meditation. I had set off doing the mindfulness of breath and body practice and zoned out completely. As automatic phrases go, there could be worse than saying to myself "May I be well, may I be happy." But what it shows up to me is that my approach to kindness meditation has become rote and sterile. I have been practising kindness meditation [as described in Chapter 3] but the phrases feel dead and have been so overused that they turned up in my mind even though I wasn't trying to do kindness meditation. It made me see how little kindness there seems to be around when I practise kindness meditation.'

It is not uncommon when we are practising meditation to feel that not much kindness is flowing. We may get impatient, wanting obvious results, and end up pushing too hard or overdoing a particular method. As when waiting for seeds to germinate, if we keep watering too much, we may end up just drowning the seeds. One tack when we are feeling stuck is to take a different approach to our meditation. That's why in this book we emphasize trying different ways to practise kindness, and outline a different approach in each chapter.

We may also benefit from easing off, not being so pushy with our meditation, and should have confidence that, if we persist in gently applying ourself, our meditation will bear fruit in time. Watching the bare branches of winter trees, we know the buds will burst when the warm spring air arrives. Although we can't see them, changes will be going on even before the first leaves appear, just as the seed starts growing, often root first, before it produces its first shoots above ground. If we are feeling despondent about our ability to experience kindness, it can help just to know that kindness is hardwired, that it is part of our make-up. So it is worth knowing something about how the brain works.

In Compassion Focused Therapy, Paul Gilbert draws on evolutionary psychology to show how compassion is integral to being human, but also how it can go wrong. Evolutionary psychology suggests that we have three main types of emotion-regulation system: threat, drive and soothing (see Table 1 opposite). The last of these, soothing, is closely linked to kindness. We shall look at each of them in turn, because knowing about the different systems can help us to understand our emotions.

Table 1: The three emotion-regulation systems

System	Emotions	Evolutionary Function
Threat	Anger Fear Disgust	Fight harder, retaliate Escape or avoid threat Avoid or expel something noxious

Drive	Wanting
	Anticipating
	Striving
	Pleasure (on achieving
	  or consummation)
		Secure rewards and
		  goals

Soothing	Calmness Contentment Affection Connectedness	Soothe or find safeness Affiliation Rest and digest

Three types of emotion regulation

Threat

The threat system is our most basic emotion system, and we share it with even simple forms of life. The function of the threat system is self-protection. When it is operating, we scan our environment for potential threats. If a threat is detected, we experience a burst of emotions such as fear, anxiety, disgust, or anger. These emotions prompt us to act, typically by running away or fighting, or they inhibit action and we freeze or submit.

The active fight-or-flight response is associated with adrenaline and the sympathetic nervous system. The passive response is associated with the primitive parasympathetic nervous system and the stress hormone cortisol. The threat system is necessary for our survival. For example, if, just as you are about to cross a road, you notice a car coming towards you at speed, you step back. The threat system is easily triggered. It needs to do this in order to protect us. It's the 'better safe than sorry' approach. The gazelle grazing on the savannah that chews lunch instead of responding to fleeting shadows coming in its direction is likely to end up as another animal's lunch.

The trouble with having an easily triggered system is that it can get overused. To some extent, how easily the threat system is triggered depends on genetics, but it is also strongly affected by our upbringing and environment. For example, if we have been brought up in an environment with lots of violence, our threat system will have been activated much of the time, leading to us having a lower threshold for threat-based emotions.

Problems such as anxiety disorders resulting from an overactive threat system are complicated by the development in humans of what is known as the 'new brain'. The 'new brain' refers to an explosion in brain matter in our evolutionary past around two million years ago. Human babies have a brain volume of 350cc at birth, but an adult has a brain volume of 1,500cc. The main increase is in the motor area and the frontal cortex. The motor area allows fine coordination, such as for texting, playing the piano, or driving a car. Some of the earliest use of this capacity in our past was probably to make tools such as stone axes. Recent discoveries have shown that the part of the brain involved in shaping something such as a stone axe is very close to the areas associated with speech. It is thought that the first speech in humans arrived when axes began to be made. The frontal cortex supports functions such as imagination, empathy, and the internalization of social rules and values. So 'new brain' functions gave rise to extraordinary new psychologies and made possible complex food production, technology, and medicine.

If the gazelle on the savannah, having spotted a potential predator, manages to escape by running away, it will return to grazing once it is out of danger. By contrast, even a minor setback can lead us to imagine a catastrophic outcome. For example, a perceived rejection can be magnified into thoughts that no one will ever love us and that we shall go through life alone. Or a fast heartbeat can be interpreted as a heart attack, and we imagine ourself dying and never seeing our loved ones again.

As far as we know, other animals, such as the gazelle, don't do this. Depression rumination, in which we go over and over the same troubling issue trying to find a solution or wondering why something has happened to us, is also an example of the threat system being overused. Thoughts that in another context might be helpful lead in this situation to worsening depression and keep us locked in a low mood.

A further complication is that we can't both flee and fight at the same time, but we can become confused about how to respond. This partly relates to our inheritance as hunter-gatherers. Whereas in fight-or-flight situations the gazelle would usually flee and a lion would normally attack, early humans could fight in bands. But they were also vulnerable to attack and might try to escape. In a contemporary social context, we might feel both anxious and angry and then become more stressed by the conflict in emotions and how to respond. Furthermore, we can end up with a layering of emotions, as shown in Figure 1 overleaf. For example, we can feel angry at feeling anxious or anxious about losing control to anger.

Drive

The drive system supports seeking out pleasures and achievements such as food, sex, comforts, friendships, status, and recognition. It produces the pleasurable feelings we experience, for example when eating a nice meal, passing an exam, or getting to date a desired person. It is associated with dopamine. Drugs that release dopamine, such as amphetamine and cocaine, produce pleasurable sensations. The function of the drive system is to motivate. When it is in balance with the other two systems, it can guide us towards important life goals.

If the drive system is blocked, which happens when we can't obtain the goal we are pursuing, the threat system is activated. We experience frustration, anger, or anxiety until we overcome the obstacle or disengage with trying to obtain the goal. Disengagement tends to lead to a dip in mood and we feel sad. The magnitude of our sadness will depend on

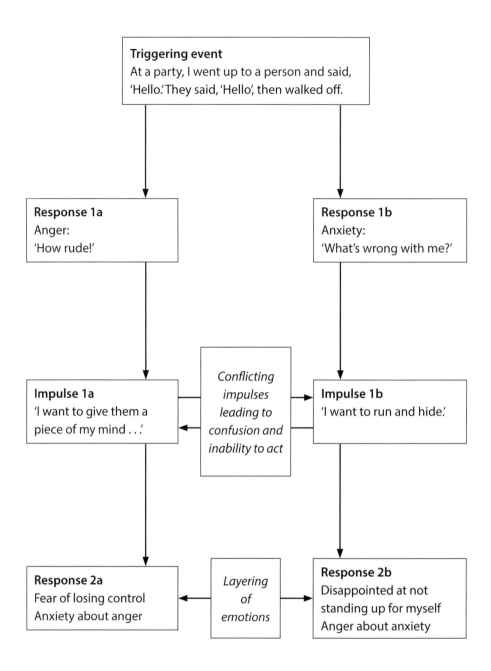

Figure 1: The layering of emotions

Mindful Emotion

how important the goal is to us. The more closely the goal is tied up with our sense of self, the greater the impact of disengaging from trying to achieve it. The strength of the rewarding nature of the drive system is illustrated by rats trained to press a lever to release cocaine into their brain: they will exhaust themselves and ignore food and drink in favour of directly stimulating the drive system by repeatedly pressing the lever.

Like the threat system, the drive system can also get out of balance. In contemporary life, with its strong emphasis on consumerism and its enormous range of choices, we can easily get caught up in constantly pursuing the latest and best objects, which leads to an unhelpful craving and sense of dissatisfaction. Rather than stopping and appreciating what we have, we can find ourself always on the go in pursuit or getting depressed by repeatedly feeling thwarted in our efforts. Depression can be associated with the continuous pursuit of unachievable goals – when we fail to disengage and to pursue more realistic ones. We can also experience depression from a thwarted drive system when we are unable to come to terms with losses such as a relationship that has ended or an illness.

Soothing

We share the first two emotion-regulation systems with fish and reptiles. These cold-blooded animals tend to produce lots of offspring, many of which will not survive into adulthood. With the shift in evolution to warm-blooded animals comes a change in strategy for raising offspring. Birds and mammals tend to produce fewer offspring but to look after them until they are capable of fending for themselves. This change in strategy is associated with a new emotion-regulation system that fosters caring between parents and offspring. The new system is particularly associated with the hormone oxytocin. In suckling, oxytocin facilitates lactation following stimulation of the nipples. Oxytocin is also associated with bonding and social behaviour and it evokes a sense of contentment and well-being. When people stroke dogs for a time, oxytocin levels increase in both the dogs and the humans.

Kindness is associated with the third emotion-regulation system. This system can help to rebalance the other two systems. We can see this in operation when a child is distressed. If the parent soothes them, the child will tend to move from the threat system to the soothing system. Repeated experiences of warmth and care like this towards the child can lead in time to the child being able to soothe themself and to balance their emotion-regulation systems themself.

When you perform an act of kindness, especially when it involves face-to-face contact with the person involved, the momentary connection between you generates oxytocin in both you and them. And when you hug someone, oxytocin flows through both of you. It is sometimes called the 'cuddle chemical', because it is produced when we hug. Kindness can also produce it, especially when it is involved in connecting with another person.

Research box: Hugs and oxytocin

An example of research looking at oxytocin and hugs is a study conducted at Chapel Hill, North Carolina in the US. It asked 59 married or partnered women to keep a diary of the number of hugs they received over a set period of time.[1] The researchers then took blood samples from each participant to analyze their level of oxytocin. It was found that women who had received more hugs had a higher level of oxytocin. They also had the lowest blood pressure and heart rate.

Knowing our emotions

It helps to be able to recognize what we are feeling and which emotion-regulation system is operating. If we notice that we are slightly anxious, it can help us to recognize that we are feeling under threat. The sense of threat might be appropriate to the situation or it could be created by our mind getting caught up in fearful fantasies or past associations. Practising mindfulness as we described in Chapter 1 can help to sharpen our awareness of subtle feelings that, if not acknowledged, can drive our behaviour in ways we may regret. If we notice that we are feeling threatened, especially when it is not appropriate to the current situation, it can help to bring some kindness to rebalance our emotions. The kindness breathing space (described on p. 66) can be a way to do this.

Written exercise: Getting to know your emotions

In order to get to know our emotion systems and gain some perspective on them, we can spend some time describing them. Take each system in turn and reflect on what it is like. What are the particular emotions that you associate with this system? If it had a colour or a shape, what would it be? When you address yourself or someone else from this system, what tone of voice does it have or what is the voice like? If you were to give it a name, what would you call it? What sort of person or animal would it be? You can use Figure 2 below to write down your answers to these questions.

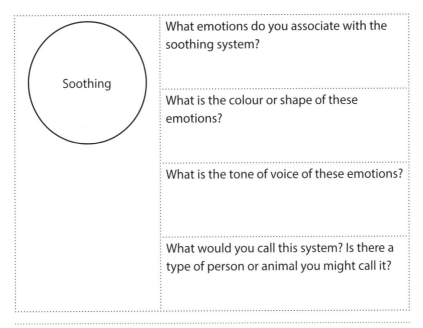

Soothing	What emotions do you associate with the soothing system?
	What is the colour or shape of these emotions?
	What is the tone of voice of these emotions?
	What would you call this system? Is there a type of person or animal you might call it?

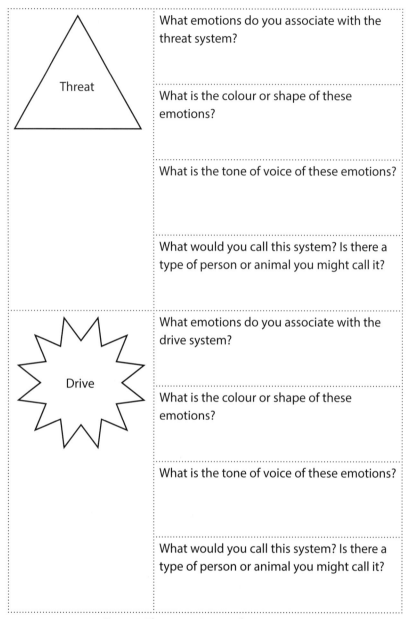

	What emotions do you associate with the threat system?
	What is the colour or shape of these emotions?
Threat	What is the tone of voice of these emotions?
	What would you call this system? Is there a type of person or animal you might call it?
	What emotions do you associate with the drive system?
Drive	What is the colour or shape of these emotions?
	What is the tone of voice of these emotions?
	What would you call this system? Is there a type of person or animal you might call it?

Figure 2: Three emotion-regulation systems

The breath and kindness

'Vagus', from the Latin *vulvivagus*, means wandering, and the vagus nerve gets its name from the way it wanders around the body in that it is the longest nerve in the body. It meanders from the brainstem down the face, innervating the muscles of the palate, pharynx, and larynx, and then goes through the major organs, including the heart, liver, lungs, stomach, intestines, and colon. Without it, not much of the body's functioning would be possible.

The vagus nerve is a component of the parasympathetic branch of the autonomic nervous system, and that system has two parts: the sympathetic and the parasympathetic. The sympathetic nervous system is associated with high-arousal negative states, such as fight-and-flight responses when the threat system is activated. By contrast, the parasympathetic nervous system more generally is thought to be responsible for activities during states of rest, such as digestion.

The breath is intimately associated with our emotional state. When we are feeling anxious or angry, our breathing tends to become more rapid and shallower. When we are feeling calm and content, our breathing tends to slow down. In mammals the vagus includes a part called the ventral vagal complex (VVC). According to Porges' polyvagal theory,[2] this portion of the vagus nerve emerged during the evolution of mammals and helps to facilitate mammalian affiliative social behaviour. Anatomically the VVC interacts with neural pathways critical to social communication and engagement behaviour. These pathways innervate the facial muscles required for emotional expression such as the muscles involved in nodding the head, a behaviour strongly associated with perceptions of social engagement with others; the muscles that orientate the head and gaze towards others; the laryngeal and pharyngeal muscles, responsible for talking and vocalizing; and the part of the middle ear that extracts the human voice from other sounds in the environment.

The action of the VVC on the heart can be observed in association with the breath. When we breathe out, the vagus nerve is working and reduces our heart rate, by inhibiting the sinoatrial node, the pacemaker, of the heart. When we breathe in, the vagus 'brake' is taken off a little and our heart rate speeds up. This moment-to-moment variation in heartbeat is called heart-rate variability. When the VVC is functioning well, there is higher heart-rate variability, which implies a more fine-tuned emotional responsiveness. This is associated with a greater ability to regulate our emotions and more behavioural adaptability. We can respond to stressful situations without excessive use of the sympathetic nervous system. Lower heart-rate variability is associated with anxiety and less behavioural flexibility. In states of high emotional arousal, the VVC is overwhelmed, and we are less able to read the emotional signals from those around us. If we are feeling extremely fearful, angry, anxious, or paranoid, self-survival predominates and we are likely to negatively misinterpret the motivations of others and to be unable to engage with them in a constructive or kindly way.

We can make use of the connection between the VVC and the breath. Deliberately slowing down the breath by paying more attention to the out-breath or by lengthening it can help to stimulate the VVC and shift us more into the soothing system. We aim to create a soothing rhythm of breath that allows our physiology to slow down. This can be helpful at moments of difficulty if we are starting to get overaroused by the threat or excitement systems. We can then better ground and focus our mind in the present moment and avoid unhelpful automatic pilot mind states.

 ## Core meditation 4: Kindness meditation using the breath (twenty minutes)

In this meditation, we use the breath as a vehicle to carry kindness. In the first stage, as we breathe in, we can imagine kindness entering the body; and as we breathe out, we try to have a sense of kindness filling the whole body. If we wish, we can imagine the breath being like a beautiful light, perhaps golden or white, like sunlight warming us or like moonlight soothing us. We can imagine the breath being soft and gentle like goosedown, fine and light as gossamer. In subsequent stages, we can imagine the breath directing kindness towards other people or imagine them breathing in and out with kindness. We could continue to imagine kindness entering us with the in-breath and then kindness going gently from us to them with the out-breath.

Preparation

Before you begin to meditate, try to spend a few minutes preparing. You might like to light a candle or some incense. If you have time, you could tidy your room a little or have a cup of tea and sit quietly.

Once you are ready, settle yourself on your cushion or chair. Bring awareness to sensations in your body, especially the contact with the ground and the chair or cushion. Take time to notice what is going on in the body and, as best you can, allow the body to settle like a sheet coming to rest on the ground.

Stage one: Self

Now bring awareness to the breath. Feel the sensation of the breath coming in and going out of the body. Without doing anything to the breath, imagine it as a stream of kindness, the body breathing kindness. If you wish, you can imagine the breath being like light, for example golden sunlight or soft white moonlight. As you breathe in and out, allow the breath to touch whatever is going on in your body or mind with a sense of acceptance, friendliness, and curiosity.

Stage two: Friend

Bring to mind a friend. Pick someone who is roughly your age, to whom you are not sexually attracted, and who is still alive. Notice what the effect is of bringing a friend to mind. You might notice sensations in the heart area or become aware of feelings or emotions. Continue to breathe as in stage one. You might also conceive a sense of your friend breathing kindness, perhaps with the light, if you find that helpful.

Stage three: Neutral person

Bring to mind a neutral person, someone you neither strongly like nor dislike. Again, notice what the effect is of bringing this person to mind. Breathe with a sense of acceptance, friendliness, and curiosity. Whenever your mind wanders off, just notice where it has gone to and then return to the breath and the neutral person.

Stage four: Difficult person

Bring to mind someone you don't like or are in conflict with. While you are new to the practice, don't choose someone you feel lots of ill will towards unless you are feeling especially kind and positive! Notice what the effect is of bringing this person to mind. Breathe with acceptance, friendliness, and curiosity towards whatever arises.

Stage five: All four people and all beings

Now bring to mind all four people: yourself, a friend, the neutral person, and the person you find difficult. Keep breathing with whatever arises. You could imagine all four people sitting together, all breathing.

Gradually expand your awareness to include all beings – as far as your imagination takes you. Imagine breathing together with all beings with a sense of acceptance, friendliness, and curiosity.

Concluding the meditation

Let go of all beings and come back to yourself. As best you can, let go of all effort. Just sit quietly breathing for a couple of minutes before bringing the meditation to an end.

Tips for working in meditation

Resting with the breath

If we develop a soothing rhythm, we are more likely to move our brain towards the part that activates the soothing system. In the first stage of kindness meditation, when we use the breath, it sometimes helps to forget about trying to cultivate kindness. We just breathe with whatever is happening. That in itself is an act of kindness towards ourself. We can use the breath to be aware of our experience. If we are struggling, feeling anxious or upset, sustained attention to the breath can soothe us.

Taking kindness into the world – the kindness breathing space with action

Our focus so far has been on practising kindness meditation. We have been training the mind in kindness. But for this to really have a transformative effect on us, we need to put kindness into action in our daily life and in our interactions with others and the environment. In the Buddhist tradition, acting with kindness and acting in ways that benefit beings, including us, is thought to help meditation and to lead to happiness. Meditation on kindness and kindly actions mutually reinforce each other. Thus this course is called Kindness *Behaviour* Training.

Strands of modern psychology also emphasize taking action as central to health and well-being. The commitment aspect of Acceptance and Commitment Therapy (ACT) means committing to valued actions. Values in ACT could take many forms and will vary between individuals, but they will be life-enhancing. Kindness would be a typical example. Studies from positive psychology show that acting on one's virtues, such as kindness, is key to being happy.

Research box: Random acts of kindness

Participants were invited to perform random acts of kindness over a period of ten weeks, such as holding open the door for a stranger or washing a flatmate's dishes. Compared to controls (who weren't asked to do acts of kindness), the participants experienced higher levels of happiness. Among the participants, some were asked to repeat the same acts each week and others to vary them. Those who were asked to perform a wider variety of acts had the highest levels of happiness.[3]

Home practice

As a first step in acting with kindness, this week we are going to practise taking our meditation out into life situations with the kindness breathing space.

Kindness breathing space with action

Just as in the meditation above, we can use the breath to extend kindness to ourself and others in the third step of the breathing space. At the end of the breathing space, we can ask ourself if there is an immediate way of acting with kindness. Here are the instructions, in three steps:

1. Notice how you are feeling right now. Check in with yourself, noticing body sensations, thoughts, and emotions.
2. Connect with the breathing. Follow the sensations of breathing without trying to do anything to the breath.
3. Extend kindness to yourself and everyone around you, either by using the breath or by using a word or phrase (as in Chapter 3), for example saying to yourself, 'May we all be free from suffering.'

Now ask yourself, 'How can I act with kindness right now?' See if something comes to mind – a kind action towards someone around you or yourself. Don't worry if nothing comes to mind. It's good to just ask the question. Something might pop up later in the day. We shall have suggestions about specific ways of acting with kindness in the coming chapters.

Also, this week try to spend fifteen to twenty minutes each day practising the kindness meditation using the breath, and at other times use the kindness breathing space.

Record on the practice record form in Table 2 below each time you practise, and remember to circle a K each time you do a kindness breathing space. In addition, make a note of anything that comes up in the practice, including any resistances to doing it, to help you reflect on the practice.

Table 2: Home practice record for chapter 4

Day / date	Kindness meditation with breath (circle)	Kindness breathing space (circle)	Comments
Day 1 Date:	Yes / no	K K K K	
Day 2 Date:	Yes / no	K K K K	
Day 3 Date:	Yes / no	K K K K	
Day 4 Date:	Yes / no	K K K K	
Day 5 Date:	Yes / no	K K K K	
Day 6 Date:	Yes / no	K K K K	
Day 7 Date:	Yes / no	K K K K	

Chapter five

···

The finest flowers:
Gratitude and generosity

Gratitude can transform common days into thanksgivings,
turn routine jobs into joy, and change ordinary opportunities
into blessings.

William Arthur Ward

At a glance

- The qualities of gratitude and generosity are closely related to kindness.
- We can appreciate our experience more fully by savouring it.
- Savouring includes luxuriating, marvelling, basking, and gratitude.
- We can boost gratitude by counting our blessings and keeping a gratitude diary.
- Some of our widely held values can block or distort gratitude and generosity, as they can with kindness.
- Generosity flows from gratitude.
- There are many things we can give, including material things, money, time, energy, and confidence.

When we walk through the park on a sunny spring morning in no hurry to get anywhere, it's hard not to be captivated by the fresh leaves opening on the trees or the sight of cherry trees in full blossom. The vibrant green unfurling leaves zing with life, the blossom dances on the branches, and all that freshness can lift your spirits. When the conditions are right, our life can deliver moments that fill us, however briefly, with joy – a streak of pink-hued dawn, the smile of a baby, the silence of first snowfall, or an unexpected postcard from a friend. Unfortunately, one of the main conditions that allows us to enjoy such moments is missing, a receptive state of mind. So often are we caught up in worries, planning, day-dreaming, or a bad mood that we scarcely register what is happening around us. We miss life. We may even stop noticing a simple pleasure such as a favourite dessert after the first mouthful.

Paying attention to the world around us and our sense experiences is an aspect of mindfulness. As we learn to recognize our mind becoming ensnared in the proliferation of thoughts, we can bring more attention back to what is in front of us. We can cultivate an attitude of savouring, that is of appreciating what is happening already, now. We get extra pleasure at no extra cost. Savouring the pleasant aspects of our experience, as well as being enjoyable in its own right, can help to counter habitual negative attitudes that are common in addiction, depression, and other mental health difficulties.

Savouring

Martin Seligmann in *Authentic Happiness* (see Appendix 2: Resources) lists four types of savouring: luxuriating, marvelling, basking, and thanksgiving.

Luxuriating

Luxuriating is savouring simple sense pleasures, such as a warm bath, a massage, or a tasty meal. However, we can pursue pleasure without really savouring. We are drawn to sense pleasure because it can give us an instant hit without too much work: for example, if we are feeling stressed, we have a drink; if depressed, we open a packet of crisps or biscuits; if bored, we browse a glossy catalogue. The problem with reaching for pleasure when we are unhappy is that it rarely solves the underlying mental state and can feed an addictive tendency.

Physical sense organs habituate: we get dwindling returns of pleasure from the same stimulus when it is repeated, and it can even become unpleasant. Thus the first chocolate in the box might taste great, the next all right, until eventually the taste of the chocolates become insipid or sickly.

Nevertheless, we can make use of sense pleasure, especially when we do it mindfully. Knowing that our sense organs habituate, we can try to vary the stimuli. For example, alternating sips of tea with eating a forkful of cake may give greater pleasure than eating the whole slice and then drinking the entire cup of tea. Also, if we approach our sense pleasures in this deliberate way, we may find that we don't need to consume so much. We can savour and stop. Mindfulness has been shown to lead to less likelihood of overeating.

What has pleasure got to do with cultivating kindness? No pleasure, and our life can feel narrow and grim, making it harder to experience kindness. Our mind will tend to contract. Experiencing pleasure can have a tonic effect on the mind, making it more likely that we shall be predisposed to feeling and acting with kindness. Pleasure can lead to a softening, relaxing, and opening up of our mind and body, and some pleasures may be more likely to lead to an opening up. Pleasure from food or sex can easily become addictive but pleasure that is associated with beauty, such as in nature, is more likely to have an elevating effect on our mind. This is the subject of our next kind of savouring, marvelling.

Marvelling

Marvelling is the appreciation of beauty, especially when we lose ourself in the moment of appreciation. We can find beauty in nature, such as when gazing at mountains or admiring a simple flower. We can enjoy the agile walk of a cat or the song of a bird. We can find beauty in art, poetry, or music. The Japanese refer to *wabi-sabi*: seeing the beauty in things that are apparently ordinary, imperfect, or even dilapidated.

Beauty tends to take us out of ourself, taking us away from unhelpful self-preoccupation. It lifts us to a larger world. The pleasure of beauty is enjoyable and less likely to fade as quickly as sense pleasures such as food. It will tend to have a refining effect on the mind, which in turn can help us to appreciate beauty more, to marvel more, creating a virtuous cycle. As beauty is pleasurable, it can be a good way to engage the mind (we shall be coming back to this in Chapter 6 when we explore the role of beauty as a means for cultivating kindness).

Basking

Basking, as when a cat enjoys the warmth of the fireside, is savouring the pleasure of receiving praise or congratulations. Depending on our conditioning, this is something we can shy away from. Basking does not mean running about with a head so big that we cannot get through the door or believing that we are perfect in every way. It is simply acknowledging and allowing ourself to enjoy praise when it comes our way.

Our response to being praised is often complicated. We can be afraid of appearing conceited or of becoming so. If we seem to like the praise, we may be afraid that it will be taken away or used to manipulate us. We may have a negative view of ourself that seems incompatible with the praise. For any of these reasons, we can try to discount or brush off the praise. We then do a disservice both to ourself and to the person who praised us. Discounting praise means that we miss an opportunity to grow beyond our habitual view of ourself. We also dismiss the action of the person who praised us. It can be difficult to make the effort to praise another person; and to discount it, especially when it is done sincerely, can be hurtful and block communication.

Thanksgiving

Thanksgiving is the expression of gratitude for the good things in our life. The 'grate' of grateful comes from the Latin *gratus*, meaning thankful and pleasing. So gratitude implies being thankful for pleasing aspects of our lives. Grace is derived from *gratus*, and so gratitude is associated with unwarranted favour or blessings. We can distinguish between gratitude and indebtedness. The latter implies that we are under some sort of obligation to another person. Gratitude is an appreciation of objects or actions that have been freely given to us.

Gratitude allows us to celebrate the present. It magnifies positive emotions. Research on emotion shows that positive emotions wear off quickly. Our emotional systems like newness and novelty. We adapt to positive life circumstances, so that before too long the new pair of shoes, the new partner, the new home don't feel so new and exciting anymore. But gratitude makes us appreciate the value of something; and when we appreciate the value of something, we extract more benefits from it. We're less likely to take it for granted. In effect, gratitude allows us to participate more in life. We notice the positives more, and that magnifies the pleasures we get from life. Instead of adapting to goodness and then it wearing out, we look to celebrate what is going well. We spend so much time watching things – televisions, computer screens, mobile phones; but with gratitude we become greater participants in our life as opposed to spectators.

 ## Written task: Appreciating your good qualities (five minutes)

Bring to mind a friend. Now imagine that they are going to describe you to someone who doesn't know you. Remember this is your *friend* describing you. How would they describe your positive qualities? What might they notice and mention? For this exercise, just write down qualities without trying to think too much. If you want to qualify or to dismiss positive qualities that your friend might list, try at least for the moment to put aside those 'yes, but' or other qualifications. Acknowledge how you feel before starting the exercise and then notice how you feel afterwards.

This exercise can be fun, if a little uncomfortable or embarrassing, to do out loud with someone else. If you have the opportunity, each can take a few minutes to say how their friend might describe them.

Blocks to gratitude

There are only two ways to live your life. One is as though nothing is a miracle. The other is as though everything is a miracle.

Albert Einstein

Just because gratitude is good for us doesn't mean it's always easy. Practising gratitude can be at odds with some deeply ingrained habits. A number of views or attitudes can get in the way of feeling gratitude. Sometimes we may not feel gratitude because we think we have a right to whatever we have been given. For example, we might think that a shopkeeper *should* be friendly and smile at us. Whether we believe that to be the case or not, clearly the shopkeeper could be unfriendly and make our shopping experience more unpleasant. But, on the other hand, if they are friendly and we appreciate it, we are more likely to be friendly back and to reinforce the friendliness from the shopkeeper. In simple ways like this, we can help to create a happier, more pleasant world, often with little cost to us.

Another block is called a 'self-serving bias'. This is when good things happen to us and we interpret this as solely because of something we did, but when bad things happen we blame other people or circumstances. Gratitude really goes against the self-serving bias because, when we're grateful, we give credit to other people for our success. We accomplished some of it ourself, yes, but we widen our range of attribution also to say, 'Well, my parents gave me this opportunity' or 'I had teachers. I had mentors. I had siblings, peers. Other people assisted me along the way.' That's very different from a self-serving bias.

A further block to gratitude can be fear of being dependent and of being indebted to the other person. It is important to be able to differentiate between indebtedness and gratitude (see above). If we confuse them, we may think that our apparent attempts to be more grateful are just going to make us feel more

Mindful Emotion

indebted, leading to feelings of guilt or to wanting to minimize kind actions from others so that we don't have to feel indebted. Sometimes people do act with apparent generosity in order to control others, but it is still worth giving people the benefit of the doubt; and, in any case, whether or not we allow ourself to be controlled in that way is primarily up to us.

From another perspective, of course, we are indebted. As babies, we could not survive without the care of the adults who, however imperfectly, brought us up. As adults, our food, clothing, and shelter all depend in various ways on other people. Growing up and in adult life, we learn so much from others, whether from formal or informal teachers. So when we cultivate gratitude, it is not about putting ourself down with an 'I'm not worthy' attitude but instead taking pleasure from our good fortune. It is learning to see the cup half full rather than half empty, because to view life in this way has a beneficial effect for us and for others.

Finally, gratitude contradicts the 'just-world' hypothesis, which argues that we get what we deserve in life. 'Good things happen to good people; bad things happen to bad people.' But we know that life is more complicated and that indeed bad things happen to good people and vice versa. Gratitude teaches us that we get more than we deserve all the time, if only we take the time to notice. Sometimes, we are told in our culture, we deserve our good fortune, and so we are entitled to it. If we deserve everything, it makes feeling gratitude for it all the more difficult.

Count your blessings

A simple way to increase your gratitude is to note things in your life that you are grateful for. Repeated reflecting on positive aspects of your life strengthens the neural connections to positive memories, which makes it easier to retrieve them, and enhances the production of positive memories. Gratitude tends to lead to happiness, which in turn makes gratitude easier to feel, each reinforcing the other.

Research box: Counting one's blessings

Emmons and McCullough show that counting one's blessings increases subjective well-being.[1] Perhaps surprisingly, more is not necessarily better: Lyubomirsky and colleagues show that people who count their blessings once a week experience greater life satisfaction than those who count their blessings three times a week.[2] Seligman and colleagues invited people to write a letter of gratitude to someone they felt they had not properly thanked and then to give the letter to that person.[3] This produced a big increase in happiness and reduction in depression, which was maintained a month later. But writing may not always be the best medium. In a study by Watkins and colleagues, people who think about someone they are grateful to experience a greater positive mood than those who write about their benefactor.[4]

The research on gratitude can give us some clues as to how best to count our blessings. It is better to reflect on specific things that have happened recently, especially in the past twenty-four hours. You can write them down or think about them, but the important thing is to try to feel a sense of appreciation, to relive the happiness that you might have felt at the time. It can be helpful to reflect on general things in your life that you are grateful for from time to time, such as your education, your parents, your partner, or your health. But, with general things, don't do it too often, probably not more than once a week. If you reflect on general things too frequently, you can start to take them for granted or to explain them away. By contrast, it can help to bring to mind each day small, specific things, such as a smile from a friendly shop assistant or the sun shining through the trees. Some people keep a daily gratitude diary for the small positive things that they notice. Recollecting these at the end of the day can be a good way to wind down at bedtime and help us to get off to sleep.

Guided reflection: Contacting gratitude (ten minutes)

Here are three quick ways to contact a feeling of gratitude:

1. Five-finger gratitude exercise. Count on your fingers five things that you are grateful for right now. If you wish, you can write them down, and really try to relish the sense of appreciation. If you come up with more than five, even better – you don't need to stop the flow if that happens. Here is an example:
   a. A colleague brought in some home-made muffins
   b. The scent of roses after rain
   c. A smile from a pedestrian when I stopped to let them cross the road
   d. A crescent moon appearing in the early evening sky
   e. The taste of caramel and hazelnut ice cream
2. Write a letter to someone whom you feel you have not properly thanked. If you feel able to, deliver it to them in person and read it out aloud to them. If you don't feel able to do that or it isn't practical, just send it to them.
3. Bring to mind something in your life that happened, for which you are grateful. It could be some important person in your life whom you met or some life-changing event. Reflect on and, if you wish, write down your thoughts about what if this had never happened. Why might this event never have happened? Consider how surprising it is that it did happen.

Thinking outside the box

We read about a woman in Vancouver whose family developed the practice of putting money in 'gratitude jars'. At the end of the day, the family would empty their pockets and put their spare change in those jars. They had a regular reminder, a routine, to get them to focus on gratitude. Then, when the jar was full, they gave the money to a person in need or to a good cause in their community.

Practices such as this can not only teach children the importance of gratitude but also demonstrate that gratitude impels people to 'pay it forward' – to give to others in some measure as we ourself have received.

Finally, we believe it's important to think outside of the box about gratitude. Mother Teresa talked about how grateful she was to the people she was helping, the sick and dying in the slums of Calcutta, because they enabled her to grow and her spirituality to deepen. That's a very different way of thinking about gratitude – in essence gratitude for what we can give as opposed to what we receive.

Research box: Gratitude

Kashdan, Uswatte, and Julian examined the role of gratitude in post-traumatic stress disorder (PTSD) in a sample of Vietnam war veterans, including forty-two patients diagnosed with PTSD and a control group of thirty-five comparison veterans. Their findings suggested that gratitude is substantially lower in people with PTSD. For both groups, gratitude was shown to relate to greater daily self-esteem and positive emotion, above the effects of the symptoms of PTSD. This suggests that a) gratitude is lower in people with PTSD, and, b) to the extent that people with it do experience gratitude, they have better daily functioning regardless of its symptoms.[5]

Seligman and colleagues tried a number of approaches to promote positive emotions. In one study, people were instructed to go on a 'gratitude visit' – write a letter to a benefactor thanking them for a gift and read it to the benefactor in person. The participants from an internet sample were instructed to write and deliver their gratitude letter within a week. Compared to those who wrote about their early childhood memories, those who went on the 'gratitude visit' reported more happiness and less depression at the immediate post-test follow-up and the one-month follow-up. Of the other positive psychology interventions tested in this study, the 'gratitude visit' had the biggest impact.[6]

Techniques such as making gratitude lists seem to work better when people are highly motivated to participate, for instance when participants have sought out 'how to' from a self-help website, than when they are externally motivated to do so. A body of literature has emerged showing that gratitude is related to a wide variety of forms of well-being. This literature stands in contrast to work showing that huge increases in income, an indication of spending power, are needed for even modest gains in well-being. This research suggests that, instead of spending our life trying to amass ever more possessions, people would be better advised to appreciate more what they actually have.

Core meditation 5: Gratitude meditation (twenty minutes)

Gratitude can form a strong basis from which to cultivate kindness. In this meditation in five stages, we use a sense of appreciation for the good things in our life to help us cultivate kindness. Both the mental biases in depression and the deadening effect (on our awareness) of addiction can make it difficult to readily bring to mind aspects of our life for which we are grateful. Therefore it can be helpful to get into the habit, for example by regularly doing the five-finger gratitude exercise, of noting the little things in our life for which we may feel grateful, for instance fine weather or small kindnesses from friends or strangers. We can bring to mind some things that we feel grateful for just in the first stage (and then proceed as in other meditations) or keep a sense of gratitude running through all five stages.

Preparation

As we have mentioned in previous chapters, before you begin to meditate, try to spend a few minutes preparing. You might like to light a candle or some incense. If you have time, you could tidy up your room or have a cup of tea and sit quietly.

Once you are ready, settle yourself onto your cushion or chair. Bring awareness to the sensations in your body, especially the contact with the ground and the chair or cushion. Take time to notice what is going on in the body. Notice too, as best you can without any judgement, what is going on in your mind, what you are feeling, and any thoughts that are prominent.

Stage one: Self

Now bring to mind some things that you feel grateful for. They don't have to be very big (but they could be). As best you can, cultivate an attitude of appreciation for your life. If you get caught up in stories about it, especially ones that aren't helpful to you now, just note that it has happened and return to the breath or body before bringing something else to mind. Take your time. There is no hurry. Bring something to mind that you appreciate in your life and then savour it. Notice the effect of bringing it to mind.

Stage two: Friend

Bring to mind a friend. Notice what the effect is of bringing a friend to mind. Spend some time reflecting on what you appreciate about your friend. Allow yourself to feel gratitude for having that person in your life or for particular qualities that they bring to it. You might notice sensations in the heart area or become aware of other feelings or emotions. Savour the sense of spending time with your friend in your imagination and appreciating them.

Stage three: Neutral person

Bring to mind a neutral person. Notice what the effect is of bringing this person to mind. Then see if there are ways of feeling gratitude towards this person. It might be as simple as that they smile at you when you show them your train ticket for inspection or that they work long hours so that you can buy milk whenever you need it. Continue as in stage one, alternating between bringing to mind something you might feel gratitude for and sitting with whatever happens.

Stage four: Difficult person

Bring to mind someone you don't like or are in conflict with. Be aware of the effect of bringing this person to mind. Even though you experience them as difficult, there may still be things that you appreciate them for (perhaps even for the challenges they bring to you!). Alternatively you could wish that they are able to experience the simple pleasure of gratitude and appreciation in their life. Continue as in stage one, alternating between reflection and sitting with whatever happens.

If you find that you are getting overwhelmed with strong negative emotions, such as feeling ill will towards the person, then redirect attention to yourself with kindness. Try to bring an attitude of kindness towards yourself as you struggle with painful emotions. Then, when you feel able to, return to the difficult person.

Stage five: All four people and all beings

Now bring to mind all four people: yourself, a friend, a neutral person, and a person you find difficult. You could reflect that all four people have good things in their life for which they might feel grateful. You could wish that they are able to enjoy a sense of gratitude and appreciation in their life. Sit as best you can with whatever arises.

Gradually expand your awareness to include all beings – as far as your imagination will take you. You could wish that all beings experience gratitude and do not take their lives for granted. Continue to alternate between reflection and just sitting with whatever arises.

Concluding the meditation

Let go of all beings and come back to yourself. As best you can, let go of all effort. Just sit quietly breathing for a couple of minutes before bringing the meditation to an end.

Tips for working in meditation

Savouring

Sometimes in the first stage of kindness meditation, we can struggle with the idea of being kind towards ourself. We may not be feeling very kind towards ourself – perhaps the very opposite. With the gratitude version of kindness meditation, we can do our best to let go of thinking about being kind to ourself. We can just enjoy the sense of appreciation; that in itself is being kind. Watch out for undermining thoughts such as 'I should feel more gratitude; I really am ungrateful.' We can notice them and then, as best we can, let them go and return to savouring the people, objects, actions, or events that have contributed to the richness in our lives.

Generosity

> *We make a living by what we get, but we make a life by what we give.*
>
> Winston Churchill

When we are feeling gratitude, it is natural to want to give. Generosity can flow out of gratitude. We ask people on KBT courses to reflect on what it is like to receive a gift and what it is like to give. We invite you to do that now. Bring to mind when someone has thoughtfully given you a small gift (not the unwanted white elephant gift from an eccentric relative at Christmas). Notice how that feels. Now reflect on what it is like when you have given a small gift, perhaps to a friend. Both receiving and giving can feel good. Receiving can lead to feelings of gratitude and giving can produce feelings of happiness and contentment.

What we find on the KBT courses is that many people actually prefer giving to receiving. Sometimes this can be for not very good reasons, such as not feeling worthy or feeling indebted (as we described above in blocks to gratitude). These reasons aside for the moment, people often find giving pleasurable because it is a great way to connect to others. If we are feeling down or upset, acting generously can lift us out of the pit of self-preoccupation and bring us into relationship with others. It can bring us a larger perspective. As well as benefiting the recipient, giving counteracts our tendency to hold on to things and to selfishness. So generosity is a good habit to cultivate. We can almost always find a way to give a little.

What to give

There are many ways to give, and in the following paragraphs we have detailed a few ideas to stimulate your thinking on ways to be generous. We all act generously sometimes (and some are very generous), so the invitation is to find new ways to give. Perhaps the most obvious, but not to be overlooked, gift is something material. It doesn't have to be big, expensive, and flashy. There are lots of occasions when we have the chance to make a small gift. Some people have a habit of always bringing a little gift such as flowers or biscuits if they are going to visit someone. If someone you live with has been away, you could brighten their room on their return with a potted plant, a card, or some chocolate. You could bake or buy a little treat and bring it in to share with your work colleagues. You might have read a book that you think someone would enjoy or find stimulating, and so you could pass it on or buy them a copy. Some of the best gifts are when they are unexpected and have really taken into account the recipient.

Related to material things is the giving of money. Giving money allows us to contribute to something that we are unable to respond to directly. If we want to respond to a natural disaster, poverty, or an environmental campaign, we can give to a relevant charity. There may also be opportunities to give to a friend in financial need or to contribute to a whip-round for a colleague's leaving present. Some traditions have a culture of tithing, giving away 10 per cent of one's income. It can be illuminating to see how much we do give away financially and then decide to increase our percentage of giving.

We can be generous with our time and energy. The French philosopher Simone Weil puts this well in her observation that 'Attention is the rarest and purest form of generosity'. It only takes a moment to help someone with a pushchair to get off the bus or to climb some stairs. We can help someone with a task such as putting up some shelves or cutting back an overgrown tree. We can lend an ear to someone who is upset or in trouble. It's often tempting to give advice too, but we should perhaps be cautious about rushing in with our good advice unless it is being clearly requested.

Sharing is another aspect of generosity. We may have the opportunity to share our food and drink or to lend a tool or an umbrella to someone in need. We can share our knowledge and experience – the best way to get to a destination, a great hotel or campsite to stay in, a wonderful piece of music, or a fine painting. We may be able to teach others a practical skill or how to appreciate a work of art. Giving in this way can cultivate an attitude of simply wanting to give of ourself in whatever way we can. Sometimes our mere presence can be a gift. Some people can inspire confidence by how they are or bring a lightness and warmth to the atmosphere. We can give by coming along to someone's celebration or accompanying them to a hospital appointment.

When we give with an attitude of generosity, we are likely to accrue a sense of well-being. We can even give that away, or at least cultivate a desire to share our happiness with others. One more thing we can share is our wisdom. We can pass on what we have learnt through life experience or teachings from others that we have found beneficial. Or we can direct people to someone we have found to be wise or to teachings that we think might be helpful. Again, like giving advice, we need to do this judiciously, really taking into account where the person is and whether or not they wish to make use of our wisdom.

When we are rooted in a deep sense of sufficiency, often our impulse is to be useful, to be kind, to give something away. We may even feel that, as we give, something is being simultaneously given back to us.

Research box: How you spend your money

A study conducted in British Columbia asked people to keep a daily record of what they spent their money on and to rate their general level of happiness. Those who spent more money on others were happiest; those who spent the least money on others were the least happy. Giving appears to make us happier.[7]

Blocks to generosity

Like kindness itself, generosity has hurdles and masks. There are blocks that we may have to get over in order to act generously and there can be attitudes that masquerade as generosity but aren't the real thing.

We have all experienced giving that does not feel generous. Sometimes gifts come with strings attached. Sometimes we give because we feel guilty; at other times, we give to impress others and make us feel superior, proud.

Buddhists describe these sentiments as 'near enemies' of giving. These are actions that look like giving but, because of attitude, assumptions, or tone, they distort authentic moments of generosity.

One of the common fears of acting generously is that we shall overdo it. We may fear that later we shall regret giving or that we shall be so busy helping and giving to others that we neglect ourself. In KBT our intention is to be kind to both ourself and others, and so in giving we need to consider ourself too. Generally if we can't give something with a good heart, with an attitude of generosity, it is probably best not to give. However, it is easy to err too much on the side of caution. We may have a generous impulse, perhaps to give to a charity. We hear about the cause and then think, Yes, I'll give a 100 dollars or pounds to that. Within moments we might find we are thinking, well maybe fifty, or perhaps ten would be enough. Then we think, I'll do it later; and in the end we don't get round to giving at all, leaving perhaps just a trace of disquiet at a good intention not acted upon.

Sometimes we can feel compelled to give. Perhaps it's a relative's birthday or it's Christmas and we feel we ought to give something even though we don't feel like it. We could feel that giving in this situation is false because it is not spontaneous. We might choose not to give, because giving would feel inauthentic. Alternatively we could make use of the convention to give on this occasion and see if we can muster some feelings of appreciation for them and wanting to give. We could try to find or to do something that will respond to them as an individual, carving out a little time to reflect on what they might like to receive.

Knowing that we are likely to be giving something can be used as an opportunity to reflect on the person and what their likes and dislikes are, and to help us avoid giving inappropriate or unwanted gifts.

We can explore our attitudes to giving. A near enemy of giving or a mask of generosity is wanting something in return. At its worst, we are giving just to get or to control, which is not generosity. Sometimes we can feel aggrieved if the gift is not appreciated or if we receive no thanks. It is pleasant to have our gift appreciated, and we should aspire to appreciate others' generosity if we are a recipient, but true generosity is unconditional. We give just to give. Another tell-tale sign that our generosity is not completely straight is if we feel upset or annoyed if someone does not wish to receive our gift. Forcing our gifts upon others is not real generosity. If someone declines our generous impulse, we can do our best to be gracious and try not to take it personally.

As mentioned above, we can block other people's generosity through our own fear of being dependent or being controlled or by believing that we are not worthy of the generosity. There may be times when we are on the receiving end of mixed motives and the wise judgement may be to decline the apparent generosity. However, allowing others to give to us can also be a great opportunity to challenge unhelpful views we have about ourself, as well as potentially to contribute towards a culture of generosity and kindness.

Recollecting positive feelings associated with giving can help us to overcome some of the blocks to generosity. Making the effort to be generous even in some small way can turn around feelings of being morose or unhappy.

In a culture of self-obsession and greed, perhaps it is reasonable to assume that we are not encouraged to be generous. Indeed, we are often taught to acquire. What we get, we tend to keep. Yet we know that all this having and keeping is curiously unsatisfying. When we are given something freely, with no 'you scratch my back and I'll scratch yours', there is no estimate of its worth.

Bonus meditation: Starting from abundance (five minutes)

This meditation can be done as a stand-alone short meditation or as a modified kindness breathing space. It can also be done at the start of a longer meditation or as an alternative final stage to one of the other kindness meditations.

Imagine a core within you that is rich and abundant. You could imagine it as a golden or white light or a sparkling precious jewel. Imagine it or the light from it filling your whole body, so that your body is pulsing or glowing with richness and abundance. Then give it away as if it were inexhaustible. Just as a candle can light many other candles without becoming diminished, imagine the richness in you overflowing and being freely given away to others.

Home practice

1. This week try to spend fifteen to twenty minutes each day practising the core gratitude meditation. Use the record form overleaf in Table 1.
2. At other times use the kindness breathing space.
3. Keep a note of things that you appreciate in your life or start a gratitude diary (see Table 2 on p. 115) by noting three things each day. They don't need to be big things. Try to record specific events or actions; and, when you write them down, savour the memory of what it is you appreciated.
4. If you wish, try to step up your practice of generosity by some extra acts of kindness: perhaps you could send a friend a postcard or give some extra time to someone.

Table 1: Home practice record for chapter 5

Day / date	Gratitude meditation (circle)	Kindness breathing space (circle)	Comments
Day 1 Date:	Yes / no	K K K K	
Day 2 Date:	Yes / no	K K K K	
Day 3 Date:	Yes / no	K K K K	
Day 4 Date:	Yes / no	K K K K	
Day 5 Date:	Yes / no	K K K K	
Day 6 Date:	Yes / no	K K K K	
Day 7 Date:	Yes / no	K K K K	

Table 2: Gratitude diary

Day / date	Gratitude (note anything you appreciate or feel grateful for)	Thoughts and feelings (note any thoughts or feelings that arise)
Day 1 Date:		
Day 2 Date:		

Day / date	Gratitude (note anything you appreciate or feel grateful for)	Thoughts and feelings (note any thoughts or feelings that arise)
Day 3 Date:		
Day 4 Date:		

Day / date	Gratitude (note anything you appreciate or feel grateful for)	Thoughts and feelings (note any thoughts or feelings that arise)
Day 5 Date:		
Day 6 Date:		

Day / date	Gratitude (note anything you appreciate or feel grateful for)	Thoughts and feelings (note any thoughts or feelings that arise)
Day 7 Date:		

Chapter six

....

Organic imagination

The living whole is prior to the parts.
Samuel Taylor Coleridge

At a glance

- Imagination is a powerful faculty that can be harnessed to support the cultivation of kindness.
- Imagination can be hijacked by rumination and worry.
- Beauty and the creative imagination are closely linked, and so contemplating beauty can help us with the positive use of imagination.
- Feeling discontent is rife in high-stimulation, affluent societies, and it works against cultivating kindness.
- Appreciating beauty, as well as simplifying our lives, spending time doing nothing, and focusing on what is most important to us, can bring us greater contentment.

Use your imagination

The great English poet Samuel Taylor Coleridge was fascinated by imagination and its analogy to the life of a plant. He observed that 'Imaginative unity is like organic unity: a self-evolved system, constituted by a living interdependence of parts, whose identity cannot survive their removal from the whole.' So far, we have confronted the weeds of our mind and have continued our journey from sowing seeds and watching the shoots appear to enjoying the first flowers. Our plant has grown, nurtured by elements such as the breath and mindful attention, like the air and light that enable a plant to flourish.

Now we wish to add the overarching faculty of imagination to help us on our path.

Imagination, like a plant, makes itself. The plant evolves spontaneously from an internal source of energy or blueprint, and so does imagination. Imagination is a mysterious set of processes but also a tremendous force we must learn to harness. We have started to add the raw materials of breath, words and phrases, and mindful attention, and now we turn to the very fabric of our mind. The achieved structure of a plant is an organic unity. The parts could be said to be their own causes. Imagination is the faculty that organizes all our constituent parts, and its existence in the garden of our heart helps to propagate new branches, leaves, and flowers of kindness. If the imagination withers, so too will the other parts of the plant. For this reason, we need to take care of our imagination, seeing it as the faculty for further growth. Let us start with some cautionary remarks.

Introduction and some notes of caution

For those of us lucky enough to have had a portable cassette recorder (like the Walkman) when they came out, the effect seemed almost miraculous. With this new piece of kit, you could listen to your favourite album while walking in your neighbourhood or sitting on the bus. It was like being transported into a movie; it transformed your everyday experience. With a touch of beauty (the music) stimulating your imagination, you could be in a different world. In this chapter, we look at how creative use of the imagination and beauty can help us to cultivate kindness. Now many of us take our MP3 player (or Spotify on our phone) for granted. We may not notice the effect of the intoxicating power of instantly accessible music interacting with our mind, but it's a power we can attend to and profit from.

First a word of caution: for many people, the word 'imagination' can incite fear and self-judgement about one's creativity or lack of it. In fact, we are all born with the faculty of imagination, not just the so-called artists among us, and we need to learn to train it. The imagination is like a muscle that needs regular exercise for its full range to be used. So just notice if this judgement arises for you: 'I lack imagination; I'm no good at being creative.' If you notice such a story in your mind, allow it to be there and notice what effect it has on your motivation and confidence to engage with this chapter.

Take a moment to imagine your most sought-after sexual fantasy – and several may spring to mind – building that image in your mind. How vivid is it? Did you manage to bring your imagination to bear on your fantasy? And how do you feel now?

Your imagination may well now be alive and kicking. What we desire most we have no trouble imagining, even quite vividly. So herein lies our task: how do we bring that same intensity of desire to bear on imagining kindness to ourself and others?

A second note of caution: most images of people that arise in our mind are *not* high-definition photos but more like fuzzy impressionistic collages. If you think of that meal you wish to make this evening or that sexual fantasy, the image is likely to be more loose and rough than intensely rich in detail.

What is imagination?

There are many misconceptions about what the imagination is and isn't. A quick dictionary version goes something like 'the faculty or action of forming new ideas, or images or concepts of external objects not present to the senses'. Well, this helps us to realize that it is something more than what we gather up through our five senses. But it is much, much more than this. Imagination can be understood as knowledge that is not derived from the senses and reason alone. It is rather a fusion of reason with emotion that in turn creates another kind of knowledge, the imaginal faculty. We take the view that it is a vital creative force in our lives. In fact, it is the essential vehicle for transforming the mind in the direction of more and more kindness.

There are two broad approaches to how we use this faculty. One is fantasy. Suppose you are bored at work. You start to daydream about something more satisfying, say your next holiday or what you will have for lunch. All this scheming and dreaming – what effect does it have your mind? Do you feel more or less expansive?

Now suppose you imagine what you love about a close friend or your child, perhaps cultivating a sense of tenderness for the fact that they are in your life. You might even imagine one thing you love about them. What effect does this have on you? Do you feel more or less expansive?

In every moment, our mind is either expanding or contracting. When we find ourself fantasizing about getting what we want, our mind tends to contract around our fantasy, narrowing our awareness to our preferred lunch, holiday, or lover. We tend to feel sucked in, like a honey trap: our minds swarm and encircle, trying to appropriate what we don't have. Fantasy tends to reinforce our sense of separateness and keeps us fixed on what is missing from the moment.

When, for example, we imagine a close friend and what we like about them or even how we can help them in some small way, it's as if our mind literally opens up. It expands, extending beyond itself to consider the well-being of another. So creative imagination, unlike fantasy, comes alive when we try and empathize with other life (not just humans). When we get into the shoes of another, in our minds we enter into relationship. We expand, and our sense of separation loosens. Using the imaginal faculty in the creative sense, we begin to resonate and empathize with life around us more; we become less concerned with ourself in a selfish sense.

The key distinction between fantasy and the creative imagination is that the latter is not trying to get anything – we are simply appreciating what we are imagining. So whatever is most important in our life needs to live not just in the world out there but also in our imagination. Part of working with the imagination is to make us more aware of how we are always building our worlds in our imagination in everyday life.

Imagination hijacked

The good news is simply that, by asking ourself what is fantasy and what it is not, we are training our mind to notice unhelpful flights of fancy. Our foundation is always mindfulness, becoming more attuned to what our mind is up to from moment to moment.

To begin with, we need to catch the hijacking in the act. A hijacked imagination has two distinct currents.

'Chewing it over': Rumination

Have you ever noticed when you see a cow that it always seems to be chewing something? Cows must chew their food twice in order to digest it properly. They spend nearly eight hours every day chewing their cud. This and the normal chewing of food can total upwards of 40,000 jaw movements per day.

Our mind is a bit like a cow, and our version of chewing the cud is mental rumination. We seem to think that we need to chew over a problem twice and many more times more in order to digest it properly. We chew over a problem with a genuine desire to solve it. But, unlike cows, we get imaginative indigestion. To help us notice rumination, we can look out for a sense of a problem that we seem to endlessly chew over, often something that we find ourself drifting into when we are bored or daydreaming. 'What did I do to deserve this?' 'When will life get easier?' 'Why am I the only . . .' All these questions seem reasonable enough, but they tend to have one thing in common: they focus on causes and consequences instead of solutions that could improve our life.

Chewing over a problem often has the effect of narrowing our awareness, focusing again on ourself as separate, and it often tends to drift into past events that were difficult or distressing. It has a repetitive aspect, as if you can't seem to get it out of your mind. In the body, it leaves us feeling as though we are in quicksand. We immediately want to struggle and fight our way out but, as with quicksand, we seem to drop further down as we try to move again. The only solution to getting free from quicksand – one that goes against our impulse – is to spread our weight over a large surface area. We have to lay ourself down; and so it is with our mind: we need to stop struggling and lay it down. We need to notice the chewing for what it is and to be with it rather than to fight against it.

Worst-case scenarios: Worry

Much like chewing the cud, this habit is repetitive, as though the cow were still chewing after its sixth espresso. Like rumination, worry is quite addictive. As with the buzz of coffee, we may like the mental agility that worry seems to bring. We feel wired up, but worst-case worry is like having one too many coffees. We fizz, jitter, feel on edge, and often there is a frightening image that accompanies these body sensations and thoughts. The imagination can come alive with scary, blown-out-of-proportion consequences.

Let's suppose that you have to give a speech right now on a subject you know little about and that there are several hundred people waiting for you to open your mouth. What does your imagination conjure up? An image of a very sweaty you trembling or at least flushed red. What is the worst thing that could happen next? It is a seemingly natural tendency we have to imagine worst-case scenarios, and often it is so automatic that we are better off accepting that we shall continue do it from time to time. As with rumination, we first need to notice and to accept that we are worrying.

We can then ask, what effect is it having on our body? For example, rumination is likely to leave us feeling slow, heavy, and lacking energy. But a typical effect of worry is feeling on edge, like we have butterflies in the stomach, are sweaty, or are struggling to concentrate.

Once we notice the effect on the body, it is a short step to fully grounding our awareness more fully in the body. This can help us to slow down the mental proliferation of whys and what ifs.

A helpful start can be to push your feet hard into the floor. Feel the ground beneath your feet and keep your feet firmly pressed on the floor. Notice if your mind keeps pulling you somewhere else. Take a few longer breaths, allowing the shoulders to drop as you breathe out. Once we are more embodied, we use this as a platform to engage the imagination more creatively. We shall explore how to do this in the next section, on beauty. Having explored the hijacked imagination, we can turn our attention to our potential, an illumined imagination.

In sum, we are suggesting that we have an imaginal faculty and that it is helpful to think of imagination as part of us – not something we have but something we are. We are encouraging a view of imagination as a potential that we can discover and develop in the direction of kindness. Like a plant, the imagination can't be fed any old rubbish. Our capacity to imagine is tremendous, and so we need to feed it with content that will help us to expand, broaden, and empathize.

Research box: Cultivating compassion

Lutz and colleagues in 2009 investigated the neural circuitry engaged in the generation of compassion by using fMRI (brain-image scanning) with fifteen novice and fifteen expert meditators. While participants engaged in a period of loving-kindness meditation, they were presented with emotional and neutral vocalizations during the brain scan. The findings suggest that cultivating the intent to be compassionate does augment empathetic responses to social stimuli, and the meditative practice of compassion may enhance our perspective, particularly with regard to the distress of others.[1]

Beauty and the imagination

We have already been using our imagination in meditation, for example imagining what the neutral person is like, and there is no end to the scope of using the imagination. In this chapter, we shall imagine a place of beauty as the basis for kindness meditation. Throughout the book, we touch on beauty, especially in nature or art. There are a number of reasons why beauty appears in a book on kindness. Firstly, it is pleasurable. Although there are dangers in getting caught up in the pursuit of pleasure, we need a degree of pleasure for our well-being. We could consider the pleasure derived from beauty in art or nature as innocent pleasure. It is less likely to feed selfish craving in the way that other forms of pleasure such as food can. If we are experiencing pleasure, it may be easier to be kind. With pleasure, we may have more psychic space and can take ourself and others in more generously.

Secondly, beauty refines the mind. Immersion in stunning scenery or an exquisite piece of music brings joy and uplifts us. This can create a mind that is more subtle and flexible – the sort of mind we need for cultivating kindness. Beauty and kindness are mutually reinforcing. With kindly eyes, we are more likely to see beauty. Even ordinary things or people whom we perhaps would not typically think of as conventionally beautiful may appear beautiful when our heart is filled with kindness. Moreover, kindness itself is beautiful. Any good act, such as a generous impulse, has a quality of beauty about it. So, in approaching kindness, we come close to beauty; and, in reflecting on beauty, we may draw close to kindness.

Thirdly, when dwelling on beauty, we are taken out of ourself. This is perhaps most obvious when beauty is awe-inspiring. With a sense of wonder, we are carried beyond our everyday concerns. Just as kindness (even though we may start with ourself) tends to expand the heart out to others, so beauty can bring us a bigger perspective beyond self-preoccupation.

Guided reflection: On beauty (five minutes)

To prepare for this week's meditation, reflect on a place of beauty. It could be a real place or an imagined one. It might be somewhere you have been on vacation or a favourite haunt from your childhood. Possible examples include being by the sea, in the mountains, or in woodland. It could be a combination of the real and the imagined, for example a sandy beach you have visited but with all the litter and noisy people removed and weather that is neither too hot nor too cold. We want to create in our mind a place in which we feel content and at ease.

As far as possible, use all your senses when imagining the place – not only what it looks like but also the sounds, smells, sensations of touch, and even tastes. So if your place were by the sea, you could imagine the expanse of turquoise water glittering in the sunshine, the sound of waves lapping on the beach, the cry of gulls, the briny smell of the sea, the feel of the sand under your feet, the breeze on your face, and the salty taste in your mouth. If you wish, write this down.

Core meditation 6: Using imagery (twenty minutes)

In this meditation we use our imagination to bring to mind a place that is unique to us where we can feel content and at ease.

We can use the reflection described above to bring to mind a place of beauty. We could allow a sense of the place being pleased that we are there, a place that wishes us well so that we can be completely at ease. It is often helpful to use the same place so that the benevolence can build up over time. Equally, we might use different places at different times depending on how we are feeling.

Preparation

Once you are ready, settle yourself onto your cushion or chair. Bring awareness to the sensations in your body, especially the contact with the ground and the chair or cushion. Take time to notice what is going on in the body. Notice too – as best you can without any judgement – what is going on in your mind, what you are feeling, and any particular thoughts that are prominent. Then spend some time with the breath, following it in and out, allowing yourself to settle more fully.

Stage one: Self

Now bring to mind a place where you can feel content and at ease. This could be a real place that you have enjoyed being in or somewhere made up in your imagination. Bring this place to mind as vividly as you can, using all the senses to create it. What does it look like? What are the sounds? How does it smell and taste? What are the sensations of your body, perhaps underfoot or on the skin? Don't worry if this is not very clear; just sense it as best you can. Imagine being in this place. And, if you wish, imagine that the place is glad that you are there and wishes you well. Notice the effect on your breath and body sensations. Notice how you feel to be there. Alternate between creating the image or sense of the place and just sitting with the effects of being in the place in your imagination.

Stage two: Friend

Bring to mind a friend. If you are comfortable in doing so, imagine your friend joining you in your special place. Allow a sense of your friend enjoying being there. Alternatively imagine your friend in a special place of their own and enjoying that. Notice what the effect is of bringing to mind your friend in your or their special place. Feel the sensations in the body, especially in the heart area. Continue as in stage one, alternating between bringing to mind your friend in the special place and sitting with whatever happens.

Stage three: Neutral person

Allow the image of your friend to fade. Return to spending a little time in your special place. Bring to mind a neutral person. If you are comfortable in doing so, imagine the neutral person joining you in your special place. Alternatively, imagine the neutral person enjoying being in their own special place. Notice what the effect is of bringing this person to mind in this way. Continue as in stage one, alternating between bringing to mind the neutral person in a special place and sitting with whatever happens.

Stage four: Difficult person

Allow the image of the neutral person to fade. Return to spending a little time in your special place. Bring to mind someone you don't like or are in conflict with. If you are comfortable in doing so, imagine this person joining you in your special place. If this seems too hard, imagine them enjoying being in their own special place. Notice what the effect is of bringing the person to mind in this way. Continue as in stage one, alternating between bringing to mind the difficult person in a special place and sitting with whatever happens.

If you find that you are getting overwhelmed with strong negative emotions, such as feeling ill will towards the person you find difficult, redirect attention to yourself with kindness. Try to bring an attitude of kindness towards yourself as you struggle with painful emotions. Then, when you feel able to, return to the difficult person.

Stage five: All four people and all beings

Allow the image of the person you find difficult to fade. Return to spending a little time in your special place. Now bring to mind all four people: yourself, a friend, the neutral person, and the person you find difficult. Imagine all four people in your special place. Know that because it is *your* special place, you can come to no harm. Alternatively you could imagine each person enjoying being in their own special place. Sit as best you can with whatever arises.

Gradually expand your awareness to include all beings – as far as your imagination will take you. You could imagine all beings joining you in your special place – its space can expand infinitely. You could wish that all beings experience the contentment and ease of being in a place of beauty and calm. Continue to alternate between a reflection and just sitting with whatever arises.

Concluding the meditation

Let go of all beings and come back to yourself. As best you can, let go of all effort. Just sit quietly breathing for a couple of minutes before bringing the meditation to an end.

Tips for working in meditation

Luxuriating in beauty

In this version of kindness meditation, we can really try to allow ourself to be in the place of beauty. We can savour and luxuriate in its beauty. Just doing this is being kind to ourself, without needing to do anything else. If it works for you, cultivate a sense that this place wants you to be there, that it is pleased that you are there.

People vary much in the vividness of their mental imagery. Some will clearly see a place of beauty in their mind's eye. Others may have more of a felt sense of the place and of what it feels like to be there. They can contact the sense of the place and just stay with that. Yet again, others prefer to use words, and so their version of the kindness meditation may be supported by dropping in an evocative word or phrase, such as 'beautiful' or 'basking in beauty'.

Contentment

When we do the place of beauty version of kindness meditation, we emphasize allowing ourself to feel a sense of contentment and ease. Being in a beautiful place, especially in nature, can evoke feelings of well-being and contentment – you don't need to be anywhere else or to do anything else. The feeling of contentment creates an atmosphere in which kindness can flourish. If we are feeling happy with our lot, it is much easier to be kind.

If you did the place of beauty exercise, you may well have brought to mind a holiday destination such as a beach or mountains. Holiday plans are often a common topic of conversation with work colleagues and friends. We imagine getting away from all the stresses and hassles of work and home life and enjoying ourself, perhaps floating on the sea or walking through a forest. Of course it doesn't always work out like that. Perhaps we are late leaving work, feeling anxious about whether or not we shall get to the rail station in time. Then, when we get there, the departure is delayed for an hour, then another, and yet another. Or perhaps we arrive at the resort feeling tired and wrung out. The hotel is noisy with party revellers (there is a stag do going on), so we can't sleep. The hotel staff seem unfriendly and say they can't move us to somewhere quieter. Next day we come down with a tummy bug and it's raining – this was supposed to be a relaxing, sunny, and warm beach holiday. We are irritable and argue with our partner. Probably many of us will be able to recount our nightmare holiday or have heard about one from others.

There are many objective difficulties in this disaster scenario, but just how badly we experience it will depend on the attitude we bring to the situation. We have one set of expectations, and then, when they are not met, we feel put out, upset, or irate – certainly not content! Unfortunately modern life and the way we operate often conspire to foster discontent. So let's look at some of the causes of discontent, so that we can consider how we can bring more contentment into our life.

Why are we discontented?

Advances in technology, while bringing many benefits, can contribute to a feeling of discontent through greater choice, complexity, and stimulation. This is exacerbated by the way our minds tend to work, through comparison and through the nature of desire.

Choice

In the film *Sleepless in Seattle*, one of the main protagonists comments on buying his morning coffee. Having selected between an array of variations such as long or short, single or double shot, skinny or full fat, size and whether or not to have flavoured syrup (and then choosing which among the many flavours), he says that he comes away feeling he has started the day having made a decision! Consumer choice, the apparent great good of the free market, can bring as much suffering as happiness. The array of different brands on the shelf in a supermarket or the sheer number of clothes shops in a big city can be overwhelming. The internet magnifies the problem. There are many sites offering different versions of the same object or service and there are also pages of reviews, which can inform but confuse too through the conflicting opinions and sheer volume. Time slips away as we become caught up in surfing different internet sites or are paralysed with indecision. Eventually we make our choice, but with the uneasy feeling that maybe we haven't got the best model or the best value for money. Choice can eat away at our life, leaving us feeling discontented.

Complexity

Having abundant choice leads to greater complexity in our life. When our mind is taken up with lots of detail, it is hard to feel contented. Even the number of passwords and codes to remember can be daunting: PIN codes for credit and debit cards; lock combinations at home, at work, and for the key pad to an ageing relative's flat; and all the passwords for the various internet shopping sites, internet banking, and email at home and work.

Technology moves very quickly, making it hard to keep up for all but the youngest or most dedicated. Electronic communication also means that work life in particular can run at a hectic pace. A generation ago, internal communication by memo might have taken a day or two to arrive; but, with email or instant messaging, responses occur much faster and can involve many people simultaneously.

Stimulation

Another dimension of technological communication is the high level of input we receive. Social media can lead to distraction as we frequently check gadgets for the latest item of news, which has an almost addictive quality. We are bombarded by advertising through hoardings, magazines, and papers, as well as through electronic media. If our mind has to process high levels of input, hold lots of detail, and then navigate multiple choices and complexity, it is little wonder that we find it hard to feel contented.

Comparison

Another source of discontent is our tendency to make comparisons. Keeping up with the Joneses, or perhaps today the Kardashians, has long been recognized as a cause of suffering. The term 'affluenza' has been coined to describe some of the ill effects of consumerism whereby the pursuit of more goods, wealth, or status paradoxically leads to suffering. Studies have suggested that those who live in countries with greater wealth inequality have a higher rate of mental disorder. We tend to compare ourself with those around us; and, if there is clear evidence of some people being much better off than we are, we may be more likely to feel unhappy. However, it is not just the worse-off who suffer. Even the wealthier in a country with high income inequality are less likely to be happy than those in a country with greater equality of income.

Beyond material possessions, our mind makes comparisons about qualities, often comparisons that are unfavourable to us. Another person is better looking, more intelligent, more generous, has a better voice, is more humorous, and so on. Many of us have a tendency to make negative judgements about ourself and easily find ourself lacking when compared to others.

The nature of desire

A central insight of the Buddha is that much of our suffering stems from desire and craving, from wanting things to be other than the way they are. As soon as we want something different, whether to have something we don't have or not have something we do have, we set up a tension. The more strongly we hold on to wanting things to be a particular way, the more likely we are to suffer and to feel discontented. Wanting in itself is painful. Often we don't notice that it is painful because we are caught up in fantasizing about having the desired object or experience. We mistake the experience of wanting for the pleasure of gratification. When we can easily get what we want – a new computer or a night at the cinema with a friend – the pain of wanting hardly registers. But if we can't get what we want, such as a house that is too expensive or love that is unrequited, the suffering becomes more obvious. The painfulness of desire can also be revealed through unmet expectations. The disappointment when we are too ill to go out to something we were looking forward to, when a friend cancels on us, or when a gadget breaks down can show up barely conscious expectations and the frustration of thwarted desire.

Another layer of desire is the tendency in wanting to overestimate the positive qualities and to downplay the negative ones. This is perhaps most starkly seen in falling in and then out of love. The loved subject initially appears to be virtually perfect; but, as we get to know them better, we start to see and sometimes become very irritated or disillusioned by their imperfections. As with people, so with material objects and experiences. Coloured by desire, they can seem highly alluring in the anticipation of acquisition but then may leave us flat or disappointed once obtained. The stronger our desire, our wanting to control our experience, or our attachment to particular outcomes, the less likely we are to feel contented.

How can we cultivate contentment?

Appreciation, not acquisition

The wanting mind seeks happiness through getting – defaulting to retail therapy, putting on music or the TV as background sound, or raiding the fridge for a snack. Even at its own level, acquisition can be counterproductive. Take eating, for example.

With the ready availability of food, it is thought that in rich countries people tend to experience hunger less. When you are not hungry, food doesn't taste as good. This can lead to choosing items with strong flavours, often salty or sweet – the sort of junk food that lends itself to overeating. The result is less pleasure from eating and rising obesity.

By contrast, appreciation works against the urge to acquire. Again with food, taking time to prepare and giving attention to what we eat lead to enjoying our food more and eating less, and probably more healthily. We talked about savouring in Chapter 5. Bringing an attitude of savouring to our sense experience yields more pleasure and promotes contentment. Appreciation of beauty, whether in nature or art, also conduces to contentment. Nature doesn't lend itself so easily to acquisition: we can't take home a sunset with us, except perhaps in a snapshot, and that can never capture completely the joy of being there. Similarly, most of us are unlikely to be able to buy an original Titian to hang on the living room wall, so in the gallery we can just relax and enjoy the works of art without becoming obsessed by trying to acquire one.

Practising kindness meditation, we are likely to appreciate people more. We may increasingly notice and enjoy their positive qualities. As in the gratitude practices in Chapter 5, we can also reflect on their qualities outside meditation. This too will promote contentment, and in addition it will feed into our kindness meditation and create a virtuous circle.

Simplifying

Like kindness and appreciation, simplicity and contentment are mutually reinforcing. Clutter and complexity work against contentment. Simplifying our physical environment can have a surprisingly positive effect on our mental state. It is so easy to accumulate material possessions – clothes, books, paperwork, and sundry objects. Although some people by character seem to maintain a lean and tidy personal environment, many of us hang on to things, just in case they might be useful one day. We think we shall sort out all that stuff but somehow don't get around to it. Attics get weighed down from hasty attempts to create space.

We may have to gird our loins to make time to go through our stuff and let things go, but the unburdening effect is usually worth it. We may have to apply the two-year rule: if it hasn't been used (worn, read, or looked at) for two years, it goes. It can be easier to part with things if we can recycle them, for example through a charity shop, as we know that others will benefit. And it is better to do this while we are alive than, all too commonly, bequeathing a legacy of stuff to our our family or friends, which will take them a long and painful time to sort through.

We can go further than this and try to acquire less in the first place, so that we don't accumulate so much. We can aim to live lightly. In rich countries, we heavily overuse our share of the planet's resources. To live more simply is an act of generosity to others as well as a help to us to be more contented.

Beyond the issue of material stuff, we can think of simplifying our lives in other ways. This might include not overextending ourself through involvement in too many activities. Even finding a daily routine that works for us can make life simpler. When people first learn to meditate, they often struggle to find time for it. It can get left to be decided each day when there might be time. The result can be that the idea of meditating hangs over you with a vague sense of unease. For some, the idea of a regular routine can sound dull, but in practice it can lead to greater freedom, as our mind is not taken up with deciding when to do what or with disappointment from another day when we didn't do what we had intended to do.

Focus on what you really value

In her book *The Top Five Regrets of the Dying*, Bronnie Ware, a palliative care nurse, recorded the biggest regrets that people had at the end of their life. Chief among them was wishing that they had had the courage to live a life true to themselves rather than the life that was expected of them. Other regrets included having spent too much time working, thus missing out on family life, and not giving time and attention to friendships, thus often losing touch with good friends. With the perspective of death, it can be easier to see what is important. Driven by fear and habit, we can end up not living the life we truly wish to lead.

By contrast, if we reflect on what is most important to us, we can use that to guide our life. Recollecting that we are going to die can be a way to bring clarity to what we value, as well as a good spur to acting on our values. When we allow ourself to follow our values, our life is likely to be more satisfying and we shall have a greater sense of contentment.

Doing nothing

A great support to contentment is giving ourself time for doing nothing at all, perhaps just sitting in a chair and allowing our mind to range at will. Often there is a strong resistance to doing nothing, as we have a strong compulsion to act. There can be a busyness that keeps us from experiencing ourself fully, and there may be uncomfortable feelings that we prefer to try to avoid. Our mind may tell us that there is too much to do to sit around and do nothing or that to do so would be lazy. Even if we are not trying to keep painful feelings at bay, we can feel impelled to act by habit and by a mind that is hungry for experience. As we tend not to see the true nature of desire – we overestimate the positive aspects of a desired object or experience – we easily get drawn into pursuing the objects of our craving. Any spare moment can be an opportunity to chase pleasure.

A half-way house to ease ourself into doing nothing is to make a cup of tea and to just drink the tea, and not to read a magazine, listen to music, check our smartphone, or watch the TV as well – just the tea. We may find that we have to go through a kind of hump, a resistance to just sitting and doing nothing. Often we feel a wave of restlessness or boredom. The cup of tea can help to anchor us in place while we sit with this and settle. If we can stay with the boredom without reaching mentally or physically for some stimulation, we may find that our mind deepens. With practice, it can become increasingly enjoyable and enriching just to be. We can learn to value this open state, the feeling of our mind like a tightly twisted rope uncoiling.

Besides being a route to contentment in its own right, doing nothing supports the other means that lead to contentment. With the open perspective of just being, we are more likely to be able to see what is of value in our life, how to act on those values, and how to simplify our life. We may see more clearly the illusory nature of desire, taking some of the heat out of the pursuit of objects of desire. Finally, if we allow ourself this space, we are more likely to feel appreciation, gratitude, and kindness.

 ## Written task: On contentment (ten minutes)

Here are some quotations to do with contentment and simplicity. We invite you to read them through and to note which ones you respond to, positively or negatively. They may stimulate you to think about contentment a little differently or remind you of the importance of contentment. What could you do to bring more contentment or simplicity into your life? Write a list of five simple things:

1. _____

2. _____

3. _____

4. _____

5. _____

Contentment is not the fulfilment of what you want but the realization of how much you already have.

Anonymous

True, time is short. But that is no reason for being in a hurry.

Sangharakshita

If we had a keen vision of all that is ordinary in human life, it would be like hearing the grass grow or the squirrel's heartbeat, and we should die of that roar which is the other side of silence.

George Eliot

Simplicity means not spreading yourself around too much. . . . Simplicity . . . conduces to depth [and so] is the opposite of superficiality.

Sangharakshita

[More choice] is a major source of stress, uncertainty, anxiety – even misery.

B. Schwartz

More and more of less and less

Sangharakshita

In the seen will be merely what is seen; in the heard will be merely what is heard; in the sensed will be merely what is sensed; in the cognized will be merely what is cognized. . . . Just this is the end of suffering.

The Buddha

Live simply that others might simply live.

Elizabeth Ann Seton

Everything that we possess that is not necessary for life or happiness becomes a burden, and scarcely a day passes that we do not add to it.

Robert Brault

The greatest step towards a life of simplicity is to learn to let go.

Steve Maraboli

My greatest wealth is the deep stillness in which I strive
and grow and win what the world cannot take from me
with fire or sword.

Johann Wolfgang von Goethe

Happiness can be attained either when existence accords
with our desires or when our desires are in harmony
with existence. True, the second alternative is difficult;
but the first is impossible.

Sangharakshita

He who is not contented with what he has would not be
contented with what he would like to have.

Socrates

You don't have to justify yourself by being useful. You
yourself are the justification for your existence . . . It's a
virtue to be ornamental as well as useful.

Sangharakshita

Home practice

- This week try to spend fifteen to twenty minutes each
  day practising the kindness meditation, imagining
  being in a special place.
- At other times use the kindness breathing space.
- Try to find some quiet time to be alone or with a friend
  in which you can really appreciate what is happening,
  for example taking a walk and noticing the trees and
  the weather or appreciating a friend.

Give your comments in Table 1 overleaf.

Table 1: Home practice record for chapter 6

Day / date	Kindness meditation using imagery (circle)	Kindness breathing space (circle)	Comments
Day 1 Date:	Yes / no	K K K K	
Day 2 Date:	Yes / no	K K K K	
Day 3 Date:	Yes / no	K K K K	
Day 4 Date:	Yes / no	K K K K	
Day 5 Date:	Yes / no	K K K K	
Day 6 Date:	Yes / no	K K K K	
Day 7 Date:	Yes / no	K K K K	

Chapter seven

....

A forest of kindness

Remember that everyone you meet is afraid of something,
loves something, and has lost something.

H. Jackson Brown Jr

At a glance

- Reflecting on our common humanity with other people can be a basis for cultivating kindness.
- We share with all other beings the facts that we are going to die and that we all want to be happy and don't want to suffer.
- Our speech has a big effect, for better or worse, on those we communicate with, so it is well worth considering how to infuse it with kindness.
- Components of kind speech include truthfulness, helpfulness, and finding the most suitable time to speak.

The Man Who Planted Trees by Jean Giono is a beautiful allegorical account of a shepherd who over his lifetime planted acorns, transforming a barren valley in the Alps into a peaceful and vibrant forest. Although it was a work of fiction, the story was so strong that during the author's life many people believed it to be true. Recreating a forest is a powerful image for restoring harmony, the whole forest being a universe with interdependent wildlife. Our default outlook is to see ourself as separate and disconnected, islands unto ourself. At best we may experience a degree of alienation, but at worst this tendency can create some of the terrible atrocities that humankind commits against fellow humans and the planet.

The contrast between humanity at its worst and the harmonious image of the forest is illustrated in the work of Sebastião Salgado, movingly captured by his son Juliano Ribeiro Salgado and Wim Wenders in the documentary *The Salt of the Earth*. Salgado as a social commentator photographed some of the evils humans can do to each other. He also restored a small part of the Atlantic Forest in Brazil, creating an institute dedicated to re-forestation, conservation, and education.

We can choose to view ourself as separate and to 'look after number one' or we can recognize our connectedness in sharing this planet, as trees in a single forest. If we choose the latter, a powerful way to generate kindness towards another person is through feeling that we have things in common with them. The word 'kind' comes from the word 'kin', meaning family. We more easily feel well disposed towards those we identify as being like us or belonging to us. In this chapter, we reflect on what links us most profoundly to all other people – our common humanity. Perhaps of all the approaches to kindness that we use in the book, this one takes us most directly into relationship with other people.

One of the chief ways we connect with each other, something distinctive about humans among all species, is our sophisticated use of language, whether spoken or written. We use language all the time, and so it can be easy to forget how strongly we are affected by the spoken and written word. We touch each other through our speech, emails, texts, and other forms of communication. In this chapter, we shall give attention to our speech, including its written form, and how we can infuse it with kindness.

Common humanity as an approach to kindness

We human beings have a wonderful and bewildering diversity. People differ in their external appearance, in their shape, size, and colour. Humans differ in their tastes and preferences, their cultural habits. In London, where we live and wrote this book, over 250 languages are spoken. Such diversity brings richness, but emphasizing difference can be used to fuel fear and hatred, setting one group against another. The past century has seen this tragedy repeated too many times, and it continues to create strife in many parts of the globe.

Existential facts

Yet, despite all our differences, fundamentally we have more in common with each other than not. We are born and we shall die. Our lifespan, even if we live to 100, is brief compared to the unthinkable length of time our planet has been in existence. During our short stay of a single lifetime, we shall suffer illness; and if we don't die young we shall experience the failing of our faculties with old age. We share these existential facts of life with all other human beings.

It's easy to lose sight of these basic facts. When we are young, and even when we are not so young, we can feel as though we are going to live forever; death seems a remote possibility. It is as though we are drunk on being young. Similarly, we can get intoxicated with being healthy, until we fall ill or have an accident and our body no longer performs as we are used to it doing. Our reactions to illness and disability can be complex. We may feel outraged that our body is not working like it used to or we may feel that it isn't fair. Even with a cold, we can feel that we have entered a strange and different realm, as though we have suddenly become old, until our health returns to what we consider as how things should be. We may feel unwanted or shunned if we are ill. Sometimes people describe how friends avoid them if they have a major illness such as cancer. We can have a reaction of fear or embarrassment if confronted with the serious illness of a friend or acquaintance.

Death, at least in many rich countries, tends to be tidied away as quickly as possible; it is literally boxed up. We have many euphemisms for avoiding the discomfort of talking about death: 'he popped his clogs'; she 'departed' or 'passed away'. When someone we know dies, a response of sadness may be mixed with other emotions. Our complex reactions to dying and how we can ignore the fact of our own mortality is well expressed in *The Death of Ivan Ilyich*, a late-nineteenth-century novella by Leo Tolstoy. In the opening chapter, Ilyich's colleagues, in the privacy of their own mind, meet the news of Ilyich's death with thoughts about how his death may give them promotion and with a kind of pride and complacency that they have managed to avoid death. It is as though he has been careless to die while they have warded off death through their own cleverness.

Our discomfort and complicated responses to death and illness can make it hard to face these existential facts head on. But when we can acknowledge them as a natural and inevitable part of life, we can feel greater sympathy with each other. In her moving book *Intimate Death*, Marie de Hennezel, a psychologist working in a French hospice, describes accompanying people to the end of their life, helping them to come to terms with their life and their death. There is a sense that, in facing their death, the people she is helping become more fully alive. Reading her accounts of the end of these people's lives is moving and even uplifting.

We don't need to be dying before we reflect on death. We can use the recollection of death, our own and others' as a spur to conduct our relationships in the way we would most deeply like to. In the face of death, trivial annoyances and disputes can dissolve. Bringing death to mind can help to soften the heart when it has become hard and cool and to allow kindness to flourish.

Desires and fears

Another line of reflection that can lead us into contact with our common humanity is to bring to mind our basic desires and fears. At root, we want to be happy and we don't want to suffer. Admittedly, sometimes the way we go about trying to be happy causes happiness neither for ourself nor for those around us. For example, we may drink alcohol to boost our mood and forget our worries, only to be left with a hangover or, especially if we use alcohol more frequently, end up feeling more depressed. But we can connect with the underlying desire to be happy and unworried without necessarily going along with a particular strategy for achieving some happiness. If we bring kind awareness to any self-defeating pattern, we can usually find at its base a yearning to be happy and free from suffering.

Similarly, when other people act in ways that just seem to cause themselves pain or to hurt those in contact with them, we can try to see their root motivations. Usually when people hurt others, it is through lack of awareness of the consequences of their actions on others or because they are hurting, like a wounded animal striking out. Rarely, some people do seem to be actively malicious, yet even here we may be able to track down a desire for happiness, however perversely pursued. This does not mean that we should condone, let alone applaud, such behaviour, but it can be a way in to seeing the other person as just that – another human being fundamentally like us. With that understanding, we may be able to feel kindness and even compassion towards the person, without necessarily approving of the specific ways in which they conduct themselves.

One way of viewing others' pain-inflicting behaviour is to regard them as doing the best they can. We cannot know all the internal and external conditions that drive another's actions – we can never know the full details of someone's life, everything that has happened to them, and how that has interacted with their thoughts and emotions, hopes and dreams. Without assuming that people cannot change or act differently in the future, we can take a perspective that others are simply doing the best they can at the moment. We can hold that position lightly. We may find that it can assist us not to get so ensnared by the apparent misdeeds of others. Without losing our ability to make moral judgements, we may discover that we have more spaciousness around others' actions. We may be able to feel and act, in the face of troubling behaviour, a little kinder.

 ## Guided reflection: Working with someone we find difficult (five minutes)

Reflecting on our common humanity can be a particularly good way to work with stage four of kindness meditation, the person we find difficult. Usually with someone we find difficult, we overfocus on what we don't like about them, all the irritating or hurtful ways of their behaviour that go against the way we believe they should behave. In this way, they come to appear in our mind as increasingly different from us. The more we are able to feel what we have in common with them, the easier it is to feel sympathetic and kind towards them.

For this exercise, try to imagine a friend of the person we find difficult. You don't need to know that friend, and maybe they don't even have any friends (which, if true, might of itself elicit some compassion). Imagine the friend of the person we find difficult describing to someone who doesn't know him or her what that person is like.

Have a go now. You might like to write down your responses. Allow yourself to settle for a few moments as though preparing for meditation, or you could do a kindness breathing space. Then bring to mind a friend of the person you find difficult. See if you can use your imagination to enter into a different perspective on the difficult person. Notice what your responses are and note any body sensations that arise and how you are feeling. If you get caught up in familiar feelings of ill will, just notice them and see if you can let them go and re-establish yourself in the perspective of the friend of the person you find difficult. When you have spent a few minutes doing this, come back to yourself, feeling your breath and body before finishing.

Research box: Kindness meditation to connect to strangers

The need for social connection is a fundamental human motive, and it is increasingly clear that feeling socially connected confers mental and physical health benefits. But in many cultures societal changes are leading to growing social distrust and alienation. Hutcherson, Seppala, and Gross conducted a study in which they used a brief loving-kindness meditation exercise to examine whether or not social connection can be created with strangers in a controlled laboratory context. Compared with a closely matched control task, even just a few minutes of loving-kindness meditation increased feelings of social connection and positivity towards unknown individuals on both explicit and implicit levels. These results suggest that this easily implemented technique may help to increase positive social emotions and to decrease social isolation.[1]

Mindful Emotion

Core meditation 7: Common humanity (twenty minutes)

In this meditation, we reflect on what we have in common with other people as a means to gain perspective and to feel a sense of connection with others. In the version described here, the main emphasis is on recollecting that we all want to be happy and don't want to suffer. You can also reflect on the basic existential facts described above, for example that we are all going to die. If you choose this line of reflection, watch out for getting too gloomy. Depending on our mood at the time and on our personal biases, we can end up feeling miserable and hopeless – we are all going to die, so what's the point of anything. If you find that happening, let go of this sort of reflection and change tack. Bring yourself back to the breath and allow yourself to feel kindness towards yourself. Reflection on death is a means to an end: if it helps you to feel more kindness, use it; if it has a contrary effect, try something else.

Preparation

Once you are ready, settle yourself onto your cushion or chair. Bring awareness to the sensations in your body, especially the contact with the ground and the chair or cushion. Take time to notice what is going on in the body. Notice too, as best you can without any judgement, what is going on in your mind, what you are feeling, and any particular thoughts that are prominent. Then spend some time with the breath, following it in and out and allowing yourself to settle more fully.

Stage one: Self

Now take some time to reflect on what you have in common with other beings, for example, all beings, in their heart of hearts like me, want to be happy and do not want to suffer. At times all beings, like me, experience pain and at times they experience pleasure. Sometimes people do things that cause themselves pain and sometimes pain happens to them. In the same way, sometimes I do things that bring me pain and sometimes pain just happens to me.

If you are suffering at the moment, you could reflect that other people will be suffering in a similar way. Try to stay with a simple reflection without going off on stories or qualifications about it; and, as best you can, notice the effect of the reflection on your body and your feelings and emotions. The intention is to encourage a sense of sympathy and kindness towards yourself as a human being, like other human beings.

Stage two: Friend

Bring to mind a friend and reflect as in stage one. For example, you could reflect that your friend, like you, wants to be happy and does not want to suffer. Feel the sensations in the body, especially in the heart area. Continue as in stage one, alternating between using a reflection in relation to your friend and sitting with whatever happens.

Stage three: Neutral person

Allow the image of your friend to fade and return to yourself. Bring to mind a neutral person. Use a reflection as in stage one, for example reflecting that this person wants to be happy and does not want to suffer. Continue as in stage one, alternating between using a reflection in relation to the neutral person and sitting with whatever happens.

Stage four: Difficult person

Allow the image of the neutral person to fade and return to spending a little time with yourself. Bring to mind someone you don't like or are in conflict with. Use a reflection as in stage one, for example reflecting that this person wants to be happy and does not want to suffer and yet may engage in actions that cause them (and others) to suffer. You could reflect that this person will grow older and die, just as you will grow older and die. If you are harbouring ill will towards them, you could ask yourself if this is how you want to live your life. Continue as in stage one, alternating between using a reflection in relation to the person you find difficult and sitting with whatever happens

If you find that you are being overwhelmed with strong negative emotions such as feeling ill will towards the person you find difficult, then redirect attention to yourself with kindness. Try to bring an attitude of kindness towards yourself as you struggle with the painful emotions. Then, when you feel able, return to the person you find difficult.

Stage five: All four people and all beings

Allow the image of the difficult person to fade and return to spending a little time with yourself. Now bring to mind all four people: yourself, a friend, the neutral person, and the person you find difficult. Reflect, for example, that all four of you want to be happy and do not want to suffer. All four of you sometimes do things to cause your own unhappiness. As best you can, encourage a sense of sympathy and solidarity with yourself and the others as humans who share a common humanity. Sit as best you can with whatever arises.

Gradually expand your awareness to include all beings – as far as your imagination will take you. Reflect on your common humanity with all beings in whatever way resonates with you. As best you can, feel a sense of sympathy, solidarity, and kindness with yourself and other beings. Continue to alternate between reflection and just sitting with whatever arises.

Concluding the meditation

Let go of all beings and come back to yourself. As best you can, let go of all effort. Just sit quietly breathing for a couple of minutes before bringing the meditation to an end.

Tips for working in meditation

Recollecting people with similar difficulties

If you find yourself struggling with difficult experiences, whether physical illness, painful emotions, or memories, reflections on common humanity can be a good way to work with the first stage. We can bring to mind others who have experienced similar difficulties. It is easy to believe that we are the only one in the world who is having a hard time. We might not express that in a conscious way, but somewhere we can feel that it is only poor old me who is suffering – no one else has it so bad! We might find ourself thinking, why me? This sort of rumination tends to make us feel worse, caught up in victim mode. So, without denying that we *are* suffering, it can be helpful to remember that so are others.

Even though each of us is a unique being, we can reflect that others have similar woes. Right now, there will be someone out there who is suffering in a similar way; and there will be those who have had similar misfortunes in the past and others who will suffer in a like manner in the future. We can try to feel sympathy with those in a similar plight.

More broadly we can know that no one, not even the apparently happiest and luckiest, can escape from suffering at some point in their life. We can see that our suffering, like theirs, is part of what it means to be human.

We may feel that we have more than our 'fair share' of suffering or misfortune in the lottery of life. If we find our mind moving in that direction, we can try to see how it is a futile line of thought that only adds to our suffering. Instead we can endeavour to use our experience of pain to help us become wiser and more compassionate. Rather than comparing our particular situation with others', we take our pain one breath at a time and know that this is just pain, that it is part of being human. To rail against it will only intensify our suffering. To stay with and acknowledge it can help us to become more fully human.

As the poet Rainer Maria Rilke puts it: 'how we squander our hours of pain . . . They are really our . . . place and settlement, foundation and soil and home.' Attended to with the right attitude, especially an attitude of kindness, we can learn from our painful experiences, and they can help us to grow.

Research box: Self-compassion meditation to improve body satisfaction

Body dissatisfaction is a major source of suffering among women of all ages. A recent study investigated whether a brief, three-week period of self-compassion meditation training would improve body satisfaction in a multigenerational group of women. Participants were randomized either to the meditation intervention group or to a waiting list control group. Results suggested that, compared to the control group, intervention participants experienced a significantly greater reduction in body dissatisfaction, body shame, and contingent self-worth based on appearance, as well as greater gains in self-compassion and body appreciation. All improvements were maintained when the participants were assessed again three months later.[2]

Kindness in speech

Plato said, 'Wise men talk when they have something to say, fools because they have to say it.' We could adapt his observation to say that the whole world is overwhelmed with the compulsion to chatter.

Much of our speech is relayed via messages in society telling us what to think, what to wear, what to eat, what to buy, and, perhaps most pervasively, what will make us happy. Much speech is motivated by a desire to shape what we want and to persuade us to buy. We like to think of ourself as a discriminating individual who decides what is and is not entering our psyche. However, the truth, as many studies have now borne out, is that many of these messages become the content of our consciousness. What is new in this technological age is the volume of content that now daily assaults our senses. Going back to Plato, we could add that all verbal communication simply mirrors the banality or profundity of the mind that provides its content. Mass media so often promote a shallowness of mind and lack the kindness and common humanity that we actually crave.

In the West, we have inherited a Cartesian worldview, a division of mind and body as separate faculties, distinct from one another. Although this view seems outdated ordinarily, we still focus on our mind as opposed to our body and tend to ignore our faculty of speech. In KBT, we are interested in the relationship of body, speech, and mind. Accordingly, speech is positioned somewhere between the world of the mind and what we do with our body (our behaviour). Speech is seen as the meeting place between our 'inner' and 'outer' worlds, thus reflecting the meeting point of our heart with the world around us. In order to infuse our speech with more kindness, we need to become more conscious of how we speak. Kindness in speech sounds 'nice enough' but this chapter aims to show that it is well worth considering how far kind speech can take us.

Awareness, listening, and silence

It might seem obvious enough but becoming more aware of others in communication means listening. Despite the deluge of words around us, there is in fact very little real communication, and often it points to a lack of listening. Without the awareness that comes from what we might call active listening, most of what we say or write is not really a communication: it is not received or taken in.

Listening is far more than registering and understanding the words being said. Perhaps we can all recall an experience of performing a kind of monologue at a friend, and in turn they monologued at us. Both of you were physically present but emotionally the words didn't quite feel received; they seemed to create a separation rather than a connection.

By active listening, we develop sensitivity in our communication. For example, when we listen to a piece of music, we listen not only to the notes but to the spaces between them too. The anticipation of the next verse, chorus, or change of key is often registered semi-consciously and even savoured. This could be analogous to listening to others, not only to the words but also to the spaces between the subtle shifts in tone of voice, the emotional atmosphere of the conversation as it unfolds. When we start to listen actively, as though we are intensely engaged with a piece of music, we start to listen to the shape of the other's body and their tone of voice. And, as well as being aware of the environment, we are listening within. This includes being attentive to the content of what is being said and also to the tone of voice, facial expression, and body language. Perhaps most often overlooked is our own emotional responses, that is, noticing if we feel subtly pleasant, unpleasant, or indifferent to the person with us. If we start to include these non-verbal cues, our conversation can become more meaningful and altogether deeper. This kind of listening becomes an act of generosity, and in many ways it communicates more than any words or responses often do.

When another person is responsive, listens well, or says something helpful, we naturally start to open up and relax. When another person is not responsive, can't hear you, or says something challenging, we naturally become tense and start to contract. In the midst of our busy lives, there will always be a flux of relative openness and relative closeness, and so it's unrealistic or potentially even unkind to expect us to be in a constant state of 'perfect communication'. But when those moments do come, and we listen more closely, we can appreciate and delight in real contact, which has at its heart a potent blend of openness and warmth. Such moments of active listening allow the person to be just as they are without us trying to shape the conversation to suit us. It is often a sign of good friendship when silence between two people feels companionable rather than awkward or terrifying.

The practice of active listening to someone else can also translate to something we can do for ourself. For example, often we can get anxious about spending quiet time alone without the smartphone or laptop nearby. If we bring the same attitude of openness to our experience 'in the gaps', this kind of companionable silence can emerge as though we are with a good friend, even though we might be alone.

Finally, we can become more receptive to 'a time and place'. We can all bring to mind something said to us that felt jarring because the context made it difficult to hear. Sometimes it's easier to bring up a tender subject with your partner when you go for a walk in nature. Or knowing a friend has recently had a bereavement, it is more difficult to be available if we meet in a busy cafe to talk about it. So it's a bit like working with the weather: we keep an eye out for good conditions that will support our ability to communicate more wholeheartedly.

In sum, we are suggesting that silence can become an active form of listening to the spaces between, more than just making the appropriate noises when someone is talking or waiting for a gap to bring ourself in. This extract below from the poem 'Keeping Quiet' by Pablo Neruda gives a flavour of the richness silence can offer.

Now we will count to twelve
and we will all keep still.

For once on the face of the earth,
let's not speak in any language;
let's stop for one second,

and not move our arms so much.
It would be an exotic moment
without rush, without engines;
we would all be together
in a sudden strangeness.[3]

What of truth?

We could see truthfulness as the foundation for kindly speech. Without it we lose the ability to trust. But what do we mean by truth? We often bemoan the lack of truth, especially from our governments and from companies that seem bent on trying to sell us something rather than telling us the facts. But how do we spot it? In order to better understand truthfulness, let us begin by looking at its opposite, false speech.

The cautionary tale of Donald Crowhurst, an amateur sailor who died during a round-the-world yacht race in 1969, dramatically illustrates the dangers of false speech. He secretly abandoned the race after encountering difficulty in the early stages. What started as a white lie about his whereabouts led to his reporting false positions throughout the race. Evidence indicates that he committed suicide after reporting false positions in an attempt to appear that he had completed the circumnavigation. Alone at sea, the pressure of the pretence he had created had tragic consequences. At the outset, he simply wanted to give himself a little advantage but eventually he found himself imprisoned in a web of self-perpetuating deceit. His experience is an extreme example of what happens when we edit the truth and it is a poignant reminder of the effects of untruth.

False speech

We can perhaps best define truthfulness by looking at untruthful or false speech. Broadly speaking, false speech falls into two categories: commission (white lies, exaggeration, understatement) and omission.

Commission

The most extreme and active form of false speech is telling an outright lie. Usually we think of a lie as simply being the direct opposite of what is true, although, of course, there are degrees of lying. Any variation from factual accuracy is to some extent false speech.

The so-called white lie is considered to be the least harmful, and indeed some view it as not a lie at all. White lies are widely employed, so it's worth looking at why we use them. Some white lies supposedly save relationships, some aim to ease a hectic situation, and others are intended to buy us time. Stretching the truth seems to be a natural component of human communication because it's the easy way out. But there are other occasions when the white lie emerges, say from fear, when it seems more likely to be unskilful. Often we hear the excuse that 'as long as we aren't hurting others or breaking the law, it's fine!' Perhaps the following list of typical white lies and why we tell them might sound familiar:

- **The table will be ready in five minutes.** Because it sounds better than fifteen minutes.
- **Oh, yeah. That makes sense.** Because option B involves admitting that I am unsure of my own view.
- **It wasn't me!** Because some things just aren't worth taking credit for.
- **Thank you so much! I just love it!** Because telling someone that I think their gift is tasteless would make me look insensitive.
- **Yeah, your hair looks great.** Even though I don't really care.
- **I'm twenty-nine.** Because saying thirty sounds like I am ten years older than twenty-nine.
- **Yeah, I'll start working on it ASAP!** Because telling you that I have other things to do first would just irritate you.
- **I thought I had already sent that email out. I'm sure I did.** Because telling you that it was a low priority and I forgot would probably hurt our relationship.

- **I'm fine.** Because to say anything more would be to admit uncomfortable feelings that I would rather not be questioned about.

If we delve into the reasons we use white lies, often it is to preserve or promote a view of how we wish to be seen in others' eyes. In essence, most of what we strive for – security, success, status, power, and praise – can be our indirect ways of trying to fill a hole within us, a hole carved out of our separation from love and our basic sense of common humanity. These strategies of indirectly winning love are like junk food: they do not deliver the real nourishment we so crave.

 Guided reflection: White lies (five minutes)

Bring to mind a recent time when you wanted to please or to be nice in an effort to avoid being hurtful. Try to bring an attitude of curiosity as to why you wanted to do this and whether or not any exaggeration, understatement, or little white lie emerged. What did you notice?

Fear of what others will think of us can subtly motivate what we say. Sometimes our primary concern may be the effect of speaking the truth in case it hurts or upsets the other person. We may feel that there is a conflict between being kind and being truthful, and sometimes we simply need to take the risk to say what we believe to be true, even if the consequences are a little messy, and particularly when we are not used to doing it.

Exaggeration and understatement are more subtle forms of false speech. We tend to exaggerate to make our fairly ordinary lives seem more colourful and exciting. At root, many of us don't really believe that we are lovable and good enough just as we are. This constant effort to inflate and embellish our lives only fuels our low self-worth further.

Understatement can have the same root cause. In wanting to please, to be nice, and to be polite, people can sometimes end up being quite false. For example, we may often say, 'We must meet up sometime' when actually we have no intention of meeting up at all. Or we might tell someone that we are not upset when actually we are. You see this sometimes in people's faces: endlessly smiling in desperation to be liked. And, actually, the desire to understate how we feel is more an attempt not to show how scared we are of being disapproved of.

Omission

When we omit things, we create a degree of untruthfulness by what we don't say. We are excessively concerned with how others will view us, and so we compensate by leaving out important elements. In effect we are misleading. We may utter something factually accurate but, as with understatement or exaggeration, we don't give the full picture. For example, someone asks us if we are going to an event they are attending and would like us to join them. We reply that we haven't booked yet, giving the impression that we are intending to book or perhaps that we haven't quite made up our mind yet. However, a more truthful response would be that we haven't booked because we have already decided that we are not going to go. Once again, our excessive concern about how others view us belies a lack of self-worth that can lead to untruthfulness.

Another area of omission is how we talk about other people and events. We can casually refer to another's shortcomings but fail to mention any good qualities or mitigating circumstances, giving an appearance that the other person is thoroughly malign or completely to blame.

Similarly, we can omit others' actions or aspects of our own behaviour in order to promote an appearance of being entirely responsible for something that went well or entirely blameless when something goes wrong. We can also do the reverse. Out of false humility, we underplay our contribution to successes and underplay the contribution of others to mishaps.

Like understatement and exaggeration, the false speech of omission is usually driven by our views about ourself. Our attachment to how we want others to view us is so strong, subtle, and pervasive that to be able to let go of these concerns while still feeling for and caring about others is a mark of real kindness.

 ## Written task: The consequences of our words (five minutes)

Think of an occasion when you have made a real effort to be truthful despite a contrary desire. How did it feel? What were the consequences? Did speaking truthfully lead to more trust and cooperation or did difficulties ensue? Use Table 1 below to reflect on and note down the consequences of false and truthful speech.

Table 1: Truthful and false speech: The consequences

What are the consequences of	
False speech	Truthful speech

Truthful speech

In general, we would see truth in speech as something that produces positive results for us and others or that leads in a positive direction. Let us work with the assumption that being truthful is the first key ingredient for kindly speech. This does not mean that we shall always achieve it but it can be a compass as we navigate towards more kindness in speech.

We also need to be sensitive and aware that speaking the truth can cause pain. On the one hand, we cannot indefinitely put off the day when we say what we know will be difficult to hear. But, on the other hand, we can't just blurt out the truth at the first possible moment. Part of the art of kindly speech is finding the best time to speak about tricky issues. And this will be helped by recognizing our default – whether we tend to be incautious or overly circumspect in approaching potentially painful topics.

In addition, we need to bring greater awareness to our intentions. As we have already seen, it is the degree of goodwill rather than good feeling that matters when training to bring about more kindness. In relation to our speech, we can try to be clear about probable motivations for false and truthful speech.

So we are starting to see that kind speech is more complex than saying nice, sweet things and suppressing difficult conversations. Bringing more awareness to what is motivating us to speak means becoming more mindful of feelings and especially the desires and/or aversions we feel towards the person we are talking to. False speech tends to undermine our efforts at connection. It's helpful to remember that false speech also often arises from a desire, underlying all motivations, for love and acceptance. But its effects unfortunately can sabotage this wish.

When we risk the truth, we are in a sense putting our heart on the line and risking disapproval and embarrassment and possibly rejection or negative judgement. Often in friendship we cover the cracks of what is shameful because we assume our vulnerability will be received as a sign of weakness. Yet, when we see our motivations for truth, we start to appreciate that sharing what makes us feel most vulnerable can actually enable us to feel more connected and loved.

In pointing up the need to bring more awareness to our speech, we are not prescribing perfection. Rather, we are encouraging the sharing of what is messy and potentially shaming in our lives, and this requires us to bring an attitude of kindness to ourself and others. It entails remembering that being people who struggle and feel insecure and incomplete is what makes us human. By inviting more truth into our speech, not only do we bring more kindness in but we also mitigate the negative effects of false speech. Often this means dropping our efforts to preserve a pretence of togetherness.

In sum, we are proposing that kindly speech is truthful speech deeply understood. As we have seen, truthfulness is much more than not telling lies. Truthfulness begins by sharing our folly as well as our qualities and our efforts to grow. Conversely, untruthfulness leads to mistrust of others and undermines our desire for connection. Truthful speech is imperative because it reflects our common humanity; it reflects the reality of our situation. When it is absent, we live out of harmony with ourself and others. If we cannot trust and confide, we limit our friendships and deny the very interconnectedness we know is true. We have summarized in Table 2 below the need to be careful with our speech. We go so far as to suggest that kind speech is both truthful and helpful but that, even then, especially if something may be difficult to hear, we need to find the right time to speak about it.

Table 2: Care in speech

	Truthful	False
Motivation to be helpful	Right timing	Avoid
Motivation to be hurtful	Avoid	Avoid

Home practice

1. This week try to spend fifteen to twenty minutes each day practising the kindness meditation reflecting on our common humanity, and record your practice and comments in Table 3 on the next page.
2. At other times use the kindness breathing space.
3. Talk to a friend and begin by mentioning an intention to speak candidly, for example saying, 'I am not used to being so honest but, as I really care about you, I want to share something that I would normally leave out.' Pick a small thing you feel ashamed of or that you have tended to avoid mentioning. Remember that to communicate with more kindness does not mean getting it right the first time round and that your motivation is for more connection and kindness.

4. Try to find an opportunity to let someone know what you appreciate about them. You could drop it into a conversation or send them a text or postcard.

Table 3: Home practice record for chapter 7

Day / date	Common humanity meditation (circle)	Kindness breathing space (circle)	Comments
Day 1 Date:	Yes / no	K K K K	
Day 2 Date:	Yes / no	K K K K	
Day 3 Date:	Yes / no	K K K K	
Day 4 Date:	Yes / no	K K K K	
Day 5 Date:	Yes / no	K K K K	
Day 6 Date:	Yes / no	K K K K	
Day 7 Date:	Yes / no	K K K K	

Chapter eight

....

The forgiving heart

To forgive is to set a prisoner free, and to discover
that the prisoner was you.

Lewis B. Smedes

At a Glance

- Forgiveness is a way to bring kindness to the experience of being hurt.
- When we hold on to grudges and resentment, it poisons our heart.
- Forgiving is a challenging practice and is to be approached gradually, but it does not mean condoning hurtful behaviour.
- Receptivity counteracts the tendency to push on in meditation and becomes increasingly important as we gain experience in meditating.
- We can take a more receptive approach by just sitting and listening to the heart and by a meditation based on kindness in the universe.

Extreme situations

Marian Partington's sister Lucy disappeared when she was 21 years old. For more than twenty years, Marian and her parents were left with the complex pain of unresolved loss. Eventually the awful truth was discovered: Lucy had been brutally murdered by Fred and Rosemary West. Understandably Marian felt intense rage and then grief at what had been done. How can one come to terms with a severe and senseless act? There were no quick fixes for Marian, but slowly and remarkably her path led her to forgiving her sister's killers. She came to recognize that, with unresolved pain, acting it out, denying it, or wishing it away it did not provide a solution. She came to realize instead that 'the only creative way forward with so much pain is to inch towards forgiving'. [1]

Hopefully we shall not be exposed to such extreme difficulty. Nevertheless, a real test of our kindness is situations in which our immediate and perhaps understandable response is one of aversion, such as when we have been hurt, let down, or betrayed by someone. There is something beautiful about forgiving as a creative response to hurt. As an aspect of kindness, forgiveness is like the fragrance of a flower. Not all flowers have scent, and often modern garden varieties have been bred for their vigour and large, brightly coloured flowers rather than for fragrance. Yet a rose without a perfume or an unscented violet seems incomplete. The Buddha likened flowers without fragrance to those who speak well but do not act on their words: all show but no action. The ability to forgive, as a dimension of kindness, brings the quality of kindness to completion, like fragrance completes the beauty of a flower.

But is it really a good idea to forgive? Are there misdemeanours that should not be forgiven? With some people, especially when they have been badly hurt, the very suggestion of the possibility of forgiveness can raise hackles and be met with scorn or outrage. Even if forgiveness seems attractive, is it not really a lofty, unattainable virtue that only truly 'spiritual' individuals can live up to? Sometimes, it can be associated with religion in the unhelpful sense of needing to purge ourself of sin. Or we may hear the sort of flippant remark that 'I forgive all the time', as if forgiveness is 'done' in a few words. So it is worth recognizing what forgiveness means to us and then to be willing to ask ourself if forgiveness is something we think is desirable and possible.

What is forgiveness?

Heroic individuals who exemplify forgiveness, from Martin Luther King to the Fourteenth Dalai Lama, are rare, not because they were endowed with a unique capacity for forgiveness but instead with a well-developed one. Forgiveness is an everyday choice, a collection of small actions that make up an attitude, and we need to start small in order to truly grasp the broader implications.

Cultivating forgiveness does mean changing our underlying personality. But we are simply trying to abide with or to come more fully into relationship with ourself and others and all the emotions that this entails. The ground for forgiveness is becoming mindful of our emotional responses to ourself and others. With anger or aversion, we are learning to let it burn itself out without compounding it further. We are learning to come into relationship with painful feelings of hurt and trusting that these feelings will burn themselves out. So often, we fuel our rage, resentment, and bitterness by looking for a hook in the world, often someone or something to blame, so as to avoid experiencing painful feelings.

At the same time, we can't force forgiveness, like squeezing the last bit of toothpaste out of the tube. We are trying to expand our capacity for kindness, especially by working with our tendency towards aversion, by including even those who have wronged us.

We can think of the second, third, and fourth stages of any kindness meditation as working with the mind's natural tendencies towards craving, indifference, and aversion respectively. In a sense, with forgiveness, we are working with our mind's tendency towards aversion. Forgiveness (for + give) literally means to give completely or without reservation. The 'for' here is derived from the Old High German, meaning thoroughly or to the utmost. So, when we forgive, we give up ill will towards someone completely, unconditionally.

Forgiveness also implies letting go of aversion when we feel that we have been injured unjustly. Sometimes we feel that to forgive someone is to condone their behaviour in some way. James Hillman, an analytical psychologist, states, 'forgiving is not a forgetting, but the remembering of wrong transformed within a wider context'.[2]

In other words, we can't just will forgiveness into being. We need to transform our aversion by putting it into a larger context. There is an aspect of surrendering our ill will and resentment without forgetting what has happened. This is not to suggest that we give up and resign our feelings and therefore condone the pain caused or the ethics of an action. To forgive is not to deny that an injustice has occurred but rather to accept a process that enables a reopening of one's heart to that person. We start to let go of hoping for the person to be different on account of our adverse feelings towards them. We can try to let things be, not struggling for the other person to be different.

Forgiveness involves giving up, as fully as possible, the resentment of seeing the other person in our narrowly defined way. Even though others might agree with you and together you decide that the person is terrible, this does not legitimize your view as somehow more objective or true. Our heart can constrict around particularly painful moments in our life and can come to define or shape the rest of it. Forgiveness is about letting the heart open to the pain rather than tightening even further. It acknowledges that this injustice is deeply painful and does not shut down to this or become overidentified with it. Forgiving can be the longer-term process and gift to ourself to move on in a healthy way. It is not a process of letting the other off the hook or of endlessly indulging in feelings of victimhood but one of turning towards the hurt with a kindness that can bear it within the broader perspective that Hillman refers to.

Where do we start?

When we have stopped recognizing any redeeming features in someone, seeing them as *all* evil or nasty, then we are lacking forgiveness. This denies our common humanity and thus needs a rebalancing emphasis of seeing their good qualities as well. How do we do this?

We can begin by placing our sense of betrayal within the much bigger frame of reference of our common humanity. This sounds simple enough; but, as we have seen throughout this book, cultivating kindness, particularly towards those we feel an aversion to, is no quick trick.

The first step is to accept that we have indeed been hurt. Yet, at the same time, it requires a willingness to let go of clinging to being hurt. So herein lies the paradox: we need to turn towards our feelings of hurt while not stoking the flames of resentment.

As children, we often learnt to carry hurt, loss, or injustice by shutting it down or by not expressing difficult feelings in order to help us deal with them. Often we did not have the language or the confidence to give voice to our feelings, particularly the ones we knew would be disapproved of or punished. Later in life, this strategy of repressing our aversive feelings for fear of being punished can get us into trouble.

The unforgiving heart

Let us look at what can happen when a painful event occurs. For example, something unpleasant happens to us or a loved one. As a consequence, we feel hurt. And we tend to have some standard responses to this.

Firstly, we can try to seek revenge. This gives rise to various emotions such as ill will and hatred, and thoughts about revenge and the ensuing emotions mutually reinforce each other. All this leads to a hardening of the heart. Secondly, we can fall into denial or avoidance of our hurt. We can try to ignore or partition off these feelings, and in the short term we might think this is working. However, we start to notice that the bitterness and resentment is seeping out in other ways and beginning to colour other relationships. For example, we start to become cynical about whether it is good ever to trust someone or we begin to talk only negatively about the person we feel hurt by, slipping into untruthful and therefore unkind speech.

Thirdly, the cynicism hardens so much that we start to question whether any sort of relationship is possible at all. We have now dug ourself into our story of hurt so much that we become convinced that the only way forward is to try to guarantee that we are never hurt again. Perhaps we start to make unrealistic demands of other people, for example laying down a rule that if their feelings for us are less than 100 per cent clear, then forget it – 'I can't trust you.' In short, we have hardened our heart from ever being hurt again.

Finally, and perhaps most perniciously, the poison well we have dug ourself can become so deep that we start to betray ourself. We talk badly about the other, perhaps seeking some sort of revenge or, conversely, denying what happened and becoming cynical. We start to betray our deepest values because we fear that we shall be hurt again, and that is too big a risk to take. Often, this self-view can take the shape of self-blame: 'I put myself at risk. I'm such an idiot, and I must not do that again' or 'I am actually to blame.' This lack of self-forgiveness is often the key that locks us out from forgiving the other person.

At the other extreme, and often with a similar underlying self-blame, we can see people who tend to describe themselves as 'victims' of life. Again, this is not to deny that we can be victims and be subject to huge levels of suffering. But, in this instance, we become so overidentified with feeling like a victim that we start to believe there is no other way to relate to life. Unfortunately sometimes people can live for years like this, holding on to some bitter pain, and often this is when forgiveness has been bypassed or has become a sour overidealistic hope that we vaguely remember once believing in.

Working with a hardened heart

When our heart hardens as a result of pain, we can ask ourself, is this how we wish to remain? Do we want our lives to be defined by wrongs done to us in the past? These can be courageous questions to ask ourself, but they are an essential preliminary step. We may need to honestly acknowledge what the possible benefits of staying 'unforgiving' are. Again, it is rare that we can honestly admit that we have not forgiven someone when it is easier to deny the pain or to suggest that we have moved on. So we need to take a forgiving tone with ourself and try to name any possible benefits we get from remaining defiant about not forgiving.

Guided reflection: Our responses to hurt (five minutes)

If we are badly hurt, what happens? You might like to bring to mind some hurt you have experienced (perhaps initially not too big a one, for the sake of this exploration) and use the diagram below to help guide your sense of understanding. We can draw out the process out in Figure 1 below. Have you experienced a hardening of the heart? What has this been like for you?

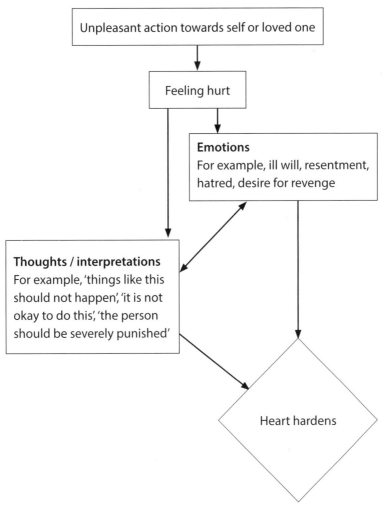

Figure 1: Hardening of the heart

Sometimes we can hold on to the pain of a past event because to let it go would seem to imply that the pain inflicted was not so bad, perhaps excusable, or even trivial. We can hold on to the pain like a badge that proves to the world how hard done by we are, and our suffering can be an indirect way of punishing the offender. If our life has in some way been defined by suffering, we may not want to let it go, as to do so would seem to invalidate as wasted all those years we have spent nursing the pain or resentment.

Written task: The benefits of not forgiving (five minutes)

Perhaps we can name a relationship that has broken down or become more distant owing to a lack of forgiveness on our part. What are the possible benefits for you of not forgiving? Often, they seem like understandable reasons, for example protecting ourself from feeling the rage we actually feel but don't know how to express or the fear that we shall be letting them off the hook.

To begin with, we can try to look at what is happening in our body response to this person. We can acknowledge how we are feeling and where we are holding these emotions in the body, for example tightness in the throat or sickness in the stomach. What are the stories about this person and the sensations in the body? (The stories are often clues about *why* we believe we are feeling sick or tight.) The stories and negative emotions are ways to protect us from the hurt. Our aim is to try to feel the hurt, bringing an attitude of kindness towards it, like a kind parent soothing an upset child and rubbing or kissing better the painful limb after a fall. We try to bring an attitude of complete attention and total sympathy towards our painful hurt. Note down all the possible benefits of remaining hardened in the heart, the narratives you tell yourself about why this person doesn't deserve to be forgiven, and any body sensations and emotions that arise when you think about them.

We can try to really feel the painful quality of all this suffering and to bring kindness to it, perhaps by trying a short kindness breathing space exercise. We can see whether or not we can soften towards some of the hardness of the ill will and resentment, as we do in the first stage of a kindness meditation. We are really acknowledging with the tenderness of a loving mother to her child that the pain we feel is just that, painful. It is unpleasant, even so unpleasant that we would rather not even feel it. We can acknowledge this – that it is OK not to like this experience – and include that too.

As with all our endeavours so far, we can then use the breath to approach these painful sensations in the body with an openness and courage to move towards them. Once we are able enough to sit with our hurt without shutting it down or feeling too overwhelmed by it, we can start to reflect on the person that caused us hurt. We can bring to mind the 'offender' and notice a part of their history that might have led them to act in the way they did. This is not to excuse or to make OK what happened, but sometimes a bit more understanding can help us to start to see their perspective a bit. We may not be able to understand the person's behaviour but we might be able to acknowledge their common humanity – they want to be loved and do not want to suffer either. You might not agree with how they express these desires but you can connect to the fact that, like you, they have done the best they could given who they were at that time. Again, to emphasize, this is not to excuse ill behaviour but to seek to bring in a little more perspective to our strongly aversive feelings towards them.

We take the view that forgiveness is a choice, an action of letting go of resentment held in the forgiver's mind. In fact, whether the perceived wrong-doing is actual or imagined, forgiveness is a choice made in the mind of the forgiver and does not condone the wrong-doing, and it frees one's mind from resentment. As long as the hurt remains unresolved, it will stimulate negative thoughts and emotions, which poison our heart and mind. It is our hope that we start to see that forgiveness serves us – it is not for the other person – and that this is okay. It is to free ourself from a mind poisoned by ill will and a body stuck in fear. We are aiming to engage more wholeheartedly with all our experience, and this includes the most challenging areas of our lives, where we feel strong dislike or aversion.

Forgiveness is a powerful antidote to aversion and connects us to our capacity for kindness. Social injustices are not going to stop and we shall be hurt and disappointed again. If we grow hard to these facts, we shut down and simply hope for the best. But, empowered with an attitude of forgiveness, we stand a chance of ensuring that our deepest ideals are not betrayed. If we are able to gain a slightly broader understanding, and especially if we are able to touch the hurt with kindness, we may be in a position to move towards forgiveness – not forgetting that this is a process, perhaps even a longer-term journey, that needs to follow the heart's pace. If the injury has been severe, it is likely to take much time. Marian Partington's journey to forgiving her sister's killers was a long one.

Guided reflection: Practising forgiveness (ten minutes)

As with all practices, we aim to start with something smaller and more manageable before moving on to larger harms when we have practised a bit more.

Begin with closing your eyes and access any aspect of kindness, perhaps using the breath to carry this quality into the body, and continue with a soothing rhythm in the belly.

We experience the hurt caused by bringing to mind someone who upset us in a way that we struggled to let go of. We need to notice this hurt in the body and, without pushing it away (aversion), come into relationship with it. What does this feel like in the body? Where in the body do you hold this hurt? Is there an image of this hurt that comes to mind?

Remember: we are working on our desire to free ourself from negative emotions, and so commit to starting to let go by gently saying, 'I forgive myself for feeling the way I do about this.' If you find yourself resisting this, see if you can extend kindness particularly to the angry part of you and again recognize the hurt caused in the body.

In this way, we are trying to hold the hurt in the context of kindness, including the angry, resentful part of ourself that feels defensive. This part needs kindness too. So again apply your soothing breath in order to honestly include these emotions.

Now imagine the person that harmed you as someone who also arrived into the world as a baby, just like you. And just like you, they did not choose the genes, the brain, or the early environment they were given. Just like you, these experiences have shaped them, and they have struggled to find their place in the world.

Bring them to mind as clearly as possible and set an intention of forgiveness by experimenting with gently saying 'I forgive you'. What makes it hard for you to forgive them? Are you frightened of letting them off the hook or letting them get away with it? If that does not feel right for you, find a warm tone of voice and look for words that feel more suitable for you, for example 'I am opening to the possibility of forgiveness'. Notice the blocks that arise when you do this. Also, remember that we are not just repeating words but are looking for the sensations in the body and cultivating a kindly, warm emotional tone to emerge as you say the words. End this exercise by letting go of this intention and just sit with your body experience, noticing what difficult emotions have arisen and again bringing as much kindness to them as possible.

Not getting our way

Forgiveness is a noble quality because it implies that, despite all the harm caused, we don't betray our aspirations to be a kinder and more compassionate human being. Despite not getting what we want, or perhaps feeling that this chapter has done nothing to shift the ill will we feel, we remind ourself that we don't betray our aspiration to cultivate kindness. It can be tempting to become disillusioned and think, 'Well, that didn't work, but I tried – so now I can go back to my old ways'. Actually, we are not doing these exercises to produce a particular outcome. Much like in the fourth stage of the kindness meditation, we need to watch out for trying to bargain with ourself. 'I've put in all this effort to be kind to you, and I can't even . . .' We need to take a longer-term view that includes the reality that we often don't get our way in life. We are always facing the fact that our mind naturally tends towards aversion, just as it naturally tends towards craving.

We might view our efforts to work with people who cause emotional discomfort as analogous to working with physical discomfort in the body. In fact, as has been the case with all mindful emotion, the body is the gateway. The more we learn to sit with physical discomfort without reacting or pushing it away, the more we can engage and sit with emotional discomfort. There is always something we can do, however small and seemingly insignificant at the time, to come more fully into relationship with our body. By learning to abide with this tendency towards aversion, by paying attention to it with kindness, we do not fuel it further but start to let it burn itself out.

We are not a limited tube from which we have to squeeze out forgiveness selectively to those we reserve it for. We can trust that, as we cultivate more qualities of kindness, we become ever larger vessels of awareness that can include even those we struggle to forgive. The bigger context we are looking to inhabit is within our mind; and, once we start to sow kindness within, we notice the world starts, perhaps in small ways, to reflect the kindness without. Our capacity to forgive can become a helpful barometer of whether we are still subtly trying to push someone else away or whether we are truly letting go of hurt. Forgiveness is a sign of the heart's maturity. Like the evocative fragrance of honeysuckle on a stroll in the quiet of a summer evening, forgiveness brings its own richness and sense of inner peace.

Research box: The benefits of forgiveness

Studies show that forgiveness is associated with less likelihood of anxiety, depression, and substance misuse, and with various positive qualities such as emotional stability and greater life satisfaction. Forgiveness also appears to have physical health benefits, and may be protective to the heart. One study, exploring the cardiovascular benefits of forgiveness, compared three groups in which people were encouraged to think about an offence with a forgiving or with an angry attitude, or were distracted.[3] All groups were then distracted for five minutes more, then were instructed to ruminate on the offence. Compared to the other groups, those who practised forgiveness significantly stopped blood pressure fluctuations, both immediately and for some time afterwards.

Mindful Emotion

Tips for working in meditation

Forgiving ourself and using fragrance

As we start to approach forgiveness as an aspect of kindness, we may discover that the main person we need to forgive is ourself. It is so easy to berate ourself for our lack of kindness and for ills that have befallen us, even when they weren't of our own making. When we sit in meditation, especially if we are struggling, we could try saying gently to ourself, 'I forgive you.' It may be helpful to bring to mind someone we think of as being kind or to imagine a kind and compassionate being, whether human or non-human. What tone of voice would they use? What would be the look in their eyes or the expression on their face? We could imagine them saying to us, 'I forgive you.' We can let the simple phrase touch us and resonate in our heart.

We have referred to forgiveness being like a fragrance. In fact, smells can have a strong and direct effect on our emotions. If we bring to mind a fragrance we like or, better still, sniff a favourite scent or perfume perhaps at the start of our meditation, it can help to soothe us and to make it a little easier to move towards forgiveness.

Activity and receptivity: Abiding in the gap

The well-known Sufi poet Rumi said, 'Your task is not to seek for love but merely to seek and find all the barriers within yourself that you have built against it.'

So far, we have seen meditation as a conscious and willed effort to cultivate different refractions of kindness. According to this approach, we could fairly assume that we have a limited capacity that we are trying to expand, as though we are trying to light a fire, something that starts as weak, flickering flames that over time and with practice become bigger and brighter.

But there is another approach to meditation. It emphasizes the unfolding of qualities that are actually inherent in our heart but that ordinarily seem more difficult to access. This latter approach entrusts our heart to take down the barriers we have built around it. Paradoxically, this clearing out is not a demolition job but a much subtler effort.

The first approach is perhaps closer to what we need in our everyday experience, and it helps particularly when we are new to meditation. But the second approach is needed as we become more confident in our practice or if we struggle with a tendency to try to force things. So often in our competitive culture, our result-driven orientation means that we push and push for success until we have cracked it, reached our goals, ticked them off, and moved on to the next challenge.

The approach of the more subtle effort is perhaps more an opening of the heart by surrender than that of a personal trainer pushing us to do that extra sit-up. This more receptive approach may be especially helpful in finding forgiveness when we need to open up to taking a bigger perspective while making efforts to remove the barnacles of a hardened heart. A forced effort with forgiveness is likely to seem like a nasty school teacher with a demanding, harsh tone of voice telling us to grow up. If we just make an effort without noticing what effect it has had, we are none the wiser about knowing how we are getting on.

A receptive approach to opening our heart tends to benefit from taking more of an attitude of surrender. Sometimes receptivity is best adopted after we have already applied more effortful activity in our meditation. It is as though we have come to the end of our workout and are just relaxing and enjoying the body feeling contented and flowing with energy and endorphins. At other times, however, we can just drop into a more receptive approach by encouraging our heart to open without the personal trainer, or the stages of the practice, and start to work more intuitively.

In all kindness meditation, we need to find a balance between activity and receptivity or between a developmental approach and an unfolding approach to meditation. One of the arts of meditation is learning to make the appropriate amount of effort. One extreme is fostering a forced will or attitude – much like an overly keen gym instructor pushing us to our limit all the time. This can produce a desire to push ourself beyond what is helpful, leading to us feeling tight, exhausted, and in meditation a bit 'heady'. The other extreme, too little effort, under the guise of 'being receptive and letting things unfold', is a sort of floppy laziness in which we just blob out in meditation. Often, we can spot this when our mind becomes more foggy or hazy, to the point of daydreaming.

There are two antidotes to this tendency to push or force our will in meditation. Firstly, we can take the view that human beings, including us, are inherently loving and kind. We imagine that our heart is already replete with riches of love and that all we need to do is to sit within this imaginative context and allow our natural kindness to unfold, a bit like a butterfly emerging from a chrysalis. For some people, this imaginative confidence in our human potential helps them to connect deeply with it; and as a result, cultivating kindness seems less an effort and more a natural response to our innate human condition.

Alternatively, we can imagine that kindness is already out there in the universe and that we simply need to open up to it. Rather than thinking that we have to pump all this kindness out into the world, we simply imagine that kindness is already there, already in bountiful supply and available to be called upon

Neither antidote is a metaphysical proposition as such, but rather a way of working with our imagination. With the first one, we find our natural human state already to be full of kindness; with the second one, the location is externalized in our imagination, to reflect a world out there that is also naturally full of kindness. Both antidotes reflect a confidence that all human beings' potential, when fully expressed, is one of kindness. Such a reflection is hard to come by in a nihilistic age in which the values of human growth are seen only to be earned or as exceptional rather than as natural and common to us all.

In thinking about this upcoming exercise, sometimes we can struggle to know what 'kindness out there or already here' means. It can seem abstract or difficult to find this idea without a felt sense or an everyday example. So, if you struggle, bring to mind a small act of kindness from your past week, for example the spontaneous smile of a stranger.

Core meditation 8: Kindness in the universe (twenty minutes)

Preparation

When you are ready, settle yourself onto your cushion or chair. Bring awareness to the sensations in your body, especially the contact with the ground and the chair or cushion. Take time to notice what is going on in the body. Notice too, as best you can without any judgement, what is going on in your mind, what you are feeling, and any thoughts that are prominent. Then give attention to the breath, following it in and out, and allow yourself to settle more fully.

Stage one: Self

Now imagine that kindness is out there in the universe. Imagine that it is already there, so you don't need to make any effort to cultivate it. Imagine it surrounding you and entering your body. If you wish, you could imagine it as light or a sense of warmth. Notice the effect of imagining that you are surrounded by kindness and that it is filling your body. Be aware of the sensations in the chest and the belly. As best you can, let yourself be open to kindness filling you from the universe. If you find that you become absorbed in thinking about it (or something else), rest your awareness on the breath or come back to body sensations.

Stage two: Friend

Bring to mind a friend. Imagine kindness from the universe surrounding and filling your friend. You could wish that they really feel the kindness and enjoy it. As you do this, feel the sensations in your body, especially in the heart area.

Stage three: Neutral person

Allow the image of your friend to fade and return to yourself. Bring to mind a neutral person. Imagine kindness from the universe surrounding and filling the neutral person. You could wish that they really feel the kindness and enjoy it. As you do this, feel the sensations in your body, especially in the heart area. As best you can, sit with whatever arises in the meditation.

Stage four: Difficult person

Allow the image of the neutral person to fade and return to spending a little time with yourself. Bring to mind someone you don't like or are in conflict with. Imagine kindness from the universe surrounding and filling both you and the person you find difficult. You could wish that you both really feel the kindness and enjoy it. As you do this, feel the sensations in your body, especially in the heart area.

Stage five: All four people and all beings

Allow the image of the difficult person to fade and return to spending a little time with yourself. Now bring to mind all four people: yourself, a friend, the neutral person, and the person you find difficult. Imagine kindness from the universe surrounding and filling all four of you. You could wish that all of you really feel the kindness and enjoy it. As you do this, feel the sensations in your body, especially in the heart area. Expand your awareness to more and more people. Imagine them surrounded by kindness from the universe and being filled by it.

Concluding the meditation

Let go of all beings and come back to yourself. As best you can, let go of all effort. Just sit quietly breathing for a couple of minutes before bringing the meditation to an end.

'Just sitting': Listening to the heart

When we are learning to meditate, we can become overly concerned with technique after a while. When things seem to dry up or to get a bit stuck, we tend to want to resolve this by trying another technique or even another practice. We can start in one direction or method, get frustrated with our progress, and head off in another, only to find another block or impasse. So we need to listen to the heart to help ground our tendency to a heady technique-orientated approach to meditation.

On the other hand, there can be wisdom in this wish to mix things up, and this book is an attempt to encourage such exploration. Some meditations might intuitively fit one person more than another. But whatever the practice, if we sincerely practise the meditations for long enough with the intention to cultivate more kindness in ourself and the world around us, we can trust that the benefits will follow.

In a sense, all we have to do is to choose a method and a place to start, and to keep working on the practice. Rather than look for a new technique, through listening to the heart, we can respond to the organic growth of our meditation practice. By 'heart', we mean here intuition, which gives a different kind of knowledge to that in our head. We need to find a way into listening to the heart, not the physical pumping organ but that deeper, more inward part of our experience that embodies such phrases as 'in my heart of hearts'. We need to find a way to listen from the heart and with the heart, from that central part of who we are.

In the *Metta Sutta*, the earliest-known Buddhist text on loving-kindness, the Buddha encourages a contemplation not of particular persons but of cultivating kindness towards beings in different geographical directions. This was no formal sitting meditation but simply a call for a constant contemplation of kindness. In a sense, whatever we are doing in meditation is simply a reminder that we have an aspiration to be kind in the world. And maybe this is enough, to constantly remind ourself through meditation that we aspire to be kinder in the world around us. Much as the *Metta Sutta* implores us to do, we are looking to develop a free-floating kindness, an attitude we carry all the time, when sitting, walking, or lying down.

In fact, we can take this contemplation a step further and imagine that we are simply listening to the heart. A 'just sitting' meditation is a bit like listening to the heart or tuning into kindness without making any effort to cultivate it. We simply rest our attention in the body and allow whatever arises in our awareness to come and go. Perhaps this approach can be viewed more like a practice of mindfulness: we are still aware of our breath and we are still primarily resting our awareness in the body around our heart area but we are not doing anything in particular. There may even be people who come to mind but we are not trying to contrive a specific outcome. We trust that our heart has a deeper, intuitive knowledge that knows how to respond and that we simply need to tune in.

This is a practice to help remind us not to get too hung up on any particular structure but rather to start to explore what the heart yearns for. So often, we hardly even register our heart as more than a bulging muscle and so often, we hardly ever think about asking it if it is okay or if it needs anything from us (speaking poetically of course). This next exercise is an opportunity to do just that – to listen and to ask our heart what it longs for.

It's important to approach this exercise, as with any meditation, without trying to achieve any result. It is about learning to be open and receptive in order to build a bridge between the everyday 'me' and the deeper core of knowing and feeling.

Bonus meditation: Listening to the heart (ten minutes)

Take your time to settle into a comfortable posture, either sitting or lying down. Find your way to tune in to your breath and your body. Feel the rhythm of your breathing and then pay particular attention to the sensations in the heart area, the centre of the chest. Is there tightness or do you find spaciousness and warmth? As best as you can, greet whatever is there with an attitude of kindness and curiosity. For a few minutes, see whether you can allow your heart to breathe, to give open attention to the heart's yearning. And, if you could put it into words, without any expectation of a response, what does your heart want or need right now?

Pose the question lightly, as far as possible letting go of any expectations, and listen to any response that might come in physical sensations, feelings, words, or images. Maybe your heart does not want to respond right now; but, as though waiting in stillness to see a shy and rare animal, try to create a light reverence in which your heart can unwind and your deeper longings unfold. Then, when you have spent some time listening to the heart and if you can, take some time before resuming your usual activities. Reflect on what your heart has to say and the implications for your life by noting down any reflections.

Conclusion

As we become more confident in meditation, with whichever method we use, the aim is to open our heart to as many people as possible, to as much of life as we can. The heart is not a tin can that needs to be wrenched open but a living organism that will contract and expand in an ever-flowing movement. 'Just sitting' practice helps us to tune in to our heart, to come to respect those natural movements while doing our best to set up conditions for it to open more. It also teaches us how to navigate the polarities of activity and receptivity, by acting as a body and imaginative anchor for our experience.

During the course, we have been trying to cultivate kindness in our heart through kindness meditation and through our actions. Even when meditation feels too much of a struggle, we can still undertake simple physical or verbal acts of kindness. Acting with kindness is a step towards happiness both for ourself and for those to whom it is directed, and our kindness meditations support us in this effort. The two mutually support and reinforce each other.

We are trying to bring kindness to all our experience: to the pleasant, the unpleasant, and the indifferent, both in relation to ourself and in relation to other people. In essence, we are trying to respond creatively to whatever happens to us. And our heart is our best ally in this endeavour.

Home practice

This week, try to spend fifteen to twenty minutes each day practising the kindness meditation based on kindness in the universe. At other times use the kindness breathing space. Record your practice and comments in Table 1 opposite.

Table 1: Home practice record for chapter 8

Day / date	Kindness in the universe meditation (circle)	Kindness breathing space (circle)	Comments
Day 1 Date:	Yes / no	K K K K	
Day 2 Date:	Yes / no	K K K K	
Day 3 Date:	Yes / no	K K K K	
Day 4 Date:	Yes / no	K K K K	
Day 5 Date:	Yes / no	K K K K	
Day 6 Date:	Yes / no	K K K K	
Day 7 Date:	Yes / no	K K K K	

Afterword

....

Fruition

You cannot do a kindness too soon, for you never know
when it will be too late.

Ralph Waldo Emerson

A Chinese proverb runs roughly thus: 'If you want to be happy
for an hour, get drunk; if you want to be happy for a day, get
married; if you want to be happy for life, plant a garden.' This
book offers ways to work on the ground of our mind, sowing
the seeds of kindness. It is just a beginning. Training our mind
and cultivating kindness is a lifetime's work, but work that
is very rewarding. Like creating a beautiful garden, the work
is satisfying in its own right, but it also brings pleasure and
happiness to others.

The fruits of kindness

The Buddha listed a number of benefits of cultivating kindness.
They include being loved and respected by others, sleeping
well, having a serene facial complexion, being protected, and
developing wisdom.

Improving our relationships with others

If we act with kindness towards others, there is no guarantee
that it will be reciprocated. If we are hoping to get some reward
for our kindly acts, we easily slip into one of the false versions
of kindness. Nevertheless, sometimes magical things happen
in our relationships when we practise kindness. Even without
consciously acting differently towards other people, we may

find that, after a period of including someone in our kindness meditation, something changes in our relationship.

Often people want their relationships to be different but we get stuck in routine patterns of relating. If one person changes, that can be enough to unfix the relationship. As with a house of cards, when you pull out a single card at the base, the whole house collapses. When we act with kindness, we give people an example of what is possible, and we may give them permission to act in a way they would most like to act. If we relate to the best in others, we are likely to see the best from them.

Sleep

A wonderful by-product of kindness is good sleep. The Buddhist tradition says that we will sleep peacefully, not have bad dreams, and wake up peacefully. When we consistently act with kindness, we have nothing to recriminate ourself with. The whirring mind that keeps us awake can settle. For this reason, it can be good to do some kindness meditation before we go to bed. We can set aside any stimulating electronic gadgets and wish ourself and others well. It can also be useful to extend kindness towards the thoughts that are keeping us alert if we find ourself lying in bed and unable to sleep.

Research box: Kindness is infectious

A study in 2010 showed that, when someone acts in a helpful, cooperative way, it affects others to three degrees of separation.[1] Surprisingly there is a knock-on effect, with the person affected by the initial helpful act going on to act in a helpful way, in turn affecting another to act helpfully and so on, three times. Moreover the tendency to act in a helpful way tends to persist over time. Even small acts of kindness can ripple out to have quite big effects.

Beautiful looks

Even the most physically beautiful person can look ugly if anger or hatred is written across their face. By contrast, someone who does not possess conventional good looks may become attractive when kindness lights up their complexion. We are hardwired to respond to kindness. From a very early age, babies will respond favourably to a smiling face. College photos of women with authentic smiles (called the Duchenne smile) predict, when followed up thirty years later, greater life satisfaction and being more likely to be happily married than their peers who in the photos have an inauthentic smile.[2]

Protection

We create the world we inhabit. If our mind is filled with suspicion and ill will, we are likely to provoke similar responses from others. We are likely to attract people who tend to dwell in those mental states – like attracts like. When we habitually act with kindness, we are less likely to draw trouble towards us. On the contrary, kindness can bring with it something of a charmed life; and when difficulties show up we may find that we still land on our feet.

As well as averting trouble from other people, kindness protects the mind. When problems do come our way, we are more resilient. Bringing kindly attention to our struggles, as opposed to allowing our mind to fill up with anxiety or resentment, we are more likely to find a solution.

Wisdom

In the heat of anger we cannot think straight. Being stirred up by negative emotions in effect makes us stupid. By contrast, the calmness of a kind and loving mind brings perspective. Kindness makes it possible to step outside our immediate small concerns and helps us to see the bigger picture.

Throughout this book, we have been emphasizing cultivating kindness towards both ourself and other people. As we continue to practise it, the distinction between self and other begins to break down. There is just kindness. Not that we can't distinguish, but the distinction becomes less and less important. When kindness fills our heart, there is no longer the desire to pick and choose in a self-orientated way. We just respond open-heartedly and with warm well-wishing to whatever we come into contact with. This can bring a tremendous sense of freedom, as we are not so driven to protect and seek out our own particular ends. At the same time, because we are not so taken by our self-preoccupations, we are more likely to see clearly and to act effectively. Kindness can open our eyes to the interconnected and interdependent nature of the world we live in and can help us to live harmoniously in it.

 ## Written task: Keeping the practice going (five minutes)

You have read the book, maybe even done a course on KBT, but the real effort and challenge are to make kindness an integral part of your life and to keep the practice of kindness going. Here are some tips to help you, and at the end of the book there is a list of resources. Before reading the tips, it might be worth pausing to review what you have learnt and what you may wish to take forward. We invite you to take a kindness breathing space and then to consider the following two questions:

A.   What are the three top insights that I have gained from KBT?

    1.   _____

    2.   _____

    3.   _____

B.   Which are the three most helpful exercises or meditations that I would like to continue to practise?

    1.   _____

    2.   _____

    3.   _____

Daily meditation practice

A daily meditation practice is the bedrock for bringing kindness more fully into our life. Many people struggle to set up a daily practice. It is better to start with something short and regular than longer and infrequent. So, even if you can manage only a few minutes each day, that will be a good foundation to build on.

You may find the downloads on our website helpful (see p. vii): you will have someone guiding you through the meditation and a pre-set length of time for it. You will find all eight core meditations there. An internet search for kindness or compassion meditation will take you to many more websites, with new ones appearing frequently, so we have given suggestions of places to look in Appendix 2: Resources. There are smartphone apps that have both led meditations and a timer function. The latter is useful when you get more experienced and don't want someone talking through the meditation.

We recommend alternating between a mindfulness meditation (as in Chapters 1 and 2) and a kindness meditation. The two mutually reinforce each other. Mindfulness meditation can help to steady the mind and counteract a tendency to busyness that sometimes occurs in kindness meditation. Kindness meditation can warm up mindfulness practices, helping to prevent them from becoming too heady and divorced from the emotions.

Go to a meditation class

It can be hard to keep up a meditation practice on your own. If you have the opportunity to attend one, a regular class can provide support and inspiration to keep your meditation going. It can be enjoyable to meditate with others: you meet like-minded people and receive input from the teachers.

Go on retreat

Retreats are an excellent way to take your meditation practice deeper. You get to leave behind some of your daily-life distractions (especially helpful for those of us with busy urban lives) and to spend more time focusing on meditation. Meditating more than once a day helps to build up a momentum that is hard to achieve at home.

There is a whole range of retreats in terms of length and level. Retreats can last a day, a weekend, two weeks, or longer. They may be aimed at people new to meditation, at those with some experience, or at those with lots of experience. Some retreats focus particularly on kindness. Look out for retreats on *mettā* (loving-kindness), compassion, or the four *brahma vihāras* (these are a family of practices related to kindness consisting of loving-kindness, compassion, sympathetic joy, and equanimity).

Reading

As noted above, we have suggestions for further reading in the resources section (Appendix 2). And, as kindness and compassion are becoming more popular, new books keep appearing. There are also websites that can provide a source of inspiration with stories of kind actions and the latest research.

Kindness in daily life

The kindness breathing space is a key practice to keep kindness alive as you go about your daily life. It is easy to underestimate the power of this simple practice. By putting in the breathing space, we start to change ingrained habits of how we respond to people and situations. Even though it may not seem much in the moment, it is like changing the course of a ship by a few degrees: over time we can end up in a very different place.

Cultivate and cherish kind friends

One of the strongest determinants of how we act is the behaviour of those around us. We like to think of ourself as self-determining individuals, but study after study shows how much we are influenced by our environment. Friends who share similar values, apart from simply being a joy in their own right, will support our endeavours to act with kindness. In the pressure of busy lives, it is easy to overlook our friends, and so it is worth making the effort to keep our friendships in good repair. It is also good to be receptive to and active in making new friends. One of the fruits of kindness, as mentioned above, is an improvement in our relationships. We may hope to see benefits in all of our relationships, but a particular delight, from mutual acts of kindness, is the blessing of true friendship.

Appendix one

....

Kindness meditation: Staying creative

In this book, we emphasize that kindness meditation is worth committing to as a daily habit long after you have finished reading this book. To keep practising is crucial to building our confidence and creativity in taking things deeper. However, we also need to be aware of warning signs that indicate a need to step back and slow down.

Signs of deepening

As we gain more experience in meditation, we may start to notice changes indicating that we are going deeper in it. We have listed some of the possible changes (the list is not exhaustive) in Table 1.

Table 1: Possible signs of deepening in meditation

Calm or stillness – our mind is a little quieter or the body feels still
Clarity – we can watch our mind more easily or follow through a line of reflection
Spaciousness – there seems to be more mental space; our mind is not so tight
Dropping down into the body – we are not so caught up in our head, and have a sense of groundedness
Contentment or bliss – we feel happy just to be sitting and meditating
Meaningful images arise – images appear in the mind's eye that feel significant

| Heightened sensory experience – sights and sounds in particular can be more vivid |
| Energy release – we may feel a tingling in the body or rushes of energy |
| Altered body sensations – our body may feel different in some ways, for example as though it is very large and expansive |

By the end of an eight-week KBT course, quite a few people will have experienced some of these signs, but by no means everybody. We vary much in terms of how our mind and body respond to meditation, so it does not mean that we are doing something wrong if we don't experience these changes. Just doing the meditation will have an effect, and often the effect appears outside the meditation rather than within it. Nevertheless, it is worth knowing about signs of deepening because, if they occur, we can gently encourage them. Generally they are pleasurable, although they can sometimes be a little frightening, as they may feel unfamiliar.

The pitfall when pleasurable states arise in meditation is that we try to grab hold of them, which is the very thing that will make them dissipate. Also, if we have had a pleasurable experience in a past meditation, we can get caught up in trying to have it again or wishing it to occur again. This will be counterproductive and likely to give rise to frustration. If we bring awareness to these experiences, without trying to do anything or to get anything, we may find they go deeper. So our job is just to notice, enjoy what is pleasurable, and let it go when it passes.

Responding to setbacks

Sometimes when we meditate we hit barriers, and this may make it difficult to practise. Below we list some of the common responses to them and suggest ways of responding. The first thing is to acknowledge with as much kindness as we can muster that these thoughts have arisen and then to use them as a cue to step back from our practice, at least while we reflect and regroup.

'It doesn't work'

It is easy to get frustrated with an apparent lack of quick results. Like pulling up a seedling to see if roots are growing, frequent looking for results is likely to be counter-productive. The practice of kindness takes time to mature and develop. So, as best we can, we develop an attitude of patience and trust in the practices – they have worked for millions of people over two millennia. Also, the effects of our practice may not appear where we expect them. Not uncommonly, kindness meditation can seem something of a struggle with apparently nothing happening, but then we find changes in our relationships with people or how we feel about them outside meditation. For example, we may find that situations that previously provoked anger no longer do so. Or it may be that we still have an initial reaction of anger but then quickly a second response emerges that is kinder, and we are able to let the anger go.

'I don't feel anything'

With kindness meditation, we can worry about not *feeling* much kindness. We might have an expectation of lovely, warm, expansive feelings. Although these might happen, they are not the most important thing. More important is having the intention or desire for kindness towards ourself and others and putting it into practical action. This is what will make a difference over the long term. People vary in how strongly they tend to experience emotions. Part of the work of cultivating kindness is simply to become more mindful of our emotions (as in the book title). Negative emotions such as anger or jealousy may make their presence felt strongly and positive emotions such as kindness may, especially if we are less familiar with them, be faint and subtle.

'I'm bored'

Often people say that they prefer the mindfulness practices to the kindness meditations: they find it hard to sustain an interest in cultivating kindness. A common scenario might be that someone brings someone to mind, feels kindness towards them, then loses interest and feels bored. They might think, 'I've directed kindness towards someone – now what do I do?' Partly this may be to do with expectations, especially, as described in the previous section, that of having strong feelings.

Boredom indicates a lack of engagement with the object, so we can try to find new ways to engage with the meditation, for example reflecting more on the qualities of the person we have brought to mind or the subtle sensations in the body associated with how we feel about them. Another approach is to ask ourself what we are interested in. Suppose it is the football results, or we are preoccupied with and worried about a future event. Can we link our preoccupation with the meditation practice, for example imagining the other person enjoying watching football with us or trying to imagine what would be their equivalent (if they don't enjoy foot-ball). In the case of anxiety, we could notice its unpleasant aspect, recognize that the other person will also feel anxiety sometimes, and wish that they come to be free from it.

Another way to work with boredom, especially if you prefer the mindfulness of breathing, is to keep an awareness of the breath going in the background. You can then move back and forth between attending to and enjoying the sensations of the breath and wishing well the person in the kindness meditation. We can use the pleasurable aspect of the breath to feed and sustain the intention of goodwill.

'It's too hard'

We all have times when meditation can be a slog. We can get stuck in rote approaches to our meditation, which leads to our practice feeling dry. It may be time to try something different or to revisit an approach to meditation we haven't used for some time. Sooner or later, we shall experience difficult thoughts, feelings, and emotions in our meditation. Taken in the right way, they can be grist to the mill of our practice. Bringing kindness towards these painful and unwanted experiences can help to transform them. With well-worn patterns this may take repeated effort and practice, but the rewards for changing ingrained unhelpful habits, or our relationship to them, are correspondingly great. Sometimes our meditation may uncover particularly distressing experiences. If you know or think that you have experienced something traumatic in the past, check out the section below on trauma.

'I'm not meditating'

We might find that we have stopped meditating without understanding why. Often it can be hard to sustain a meditation practice on our own. In the Afterword, we suggest some ideas to help set up a regular practice. It is also worth reflecting whether there are other barriers that stop us from meditating. Sometimes, if we have had a painful experience in meditation, it can put us off and we are reluctant to meditate. It may be good to take some time to regroup, to remind ourself why we wish to meditate. If on balance you feel you no longer wish to meditate, or at least not at present, then it is best to acknowledge that rather than half-intending to meditate and then giving yourself a hard time for not meditating. You may need some fresh inspiration – you will find some ideas in the resources appendix. If a particular problem has come up that is stopping you from meditating, you may find answers in the book or may benefit from going to a meditation class or seeking advice from a teacher.

Trauma

Occasionally meditation can stir up extremely difficult emotions, especially if we have experienced trauma in the past. By trauma, we mean a broad swathe of human experience that includes the death of a loved one, a road traffic accident, divorce, surgery, or being a victim of a crime or of sexual and emotional abuse. Trauma is subjective, and so this list is not exhaustive; but it is important that we make intelligent choices about how to allocate our attention and awareness in meditation.

As we open our mind and loosen old habits, we become more sensitive to the ebb and flow of our inner life. As we become more receptive to our inner currents, we are more likely to remember traumatic events from our past. Understandably, experiences of trauma lead us to develop elaborate strategies to avoid feeling the pain associated with these memories.

Here is a word of warning if you are someone who struggles to tolerate and regulate the intensity of painful feelings or who typically and repeatedly copes by escaping into distraction or acting impulsively. It might be necessary to learn mindfulness and kindness practices in the context of a therapy relationship as a first step.

Jim Hopper, a psychologist and researcher at Harvard, lists five signs in meditation that someone might not be ready to engage in regular practice:

1. A tendency to feel overwhelmed and 'flooded' by painful feelings and memories.
2. A tendency to 'dissociate'. Depersonalization or dissociation is a kind of avoidance, like a frozen lake over an unseen volcano of turmoil. Sometimes people with an emotional trauma might think they are doing something 'spiritual' by doing meditation, but they may simply be finding another way to escape feeling all the messages their body and their emotions are trying to convey.
3. A tendency to view meditation practice as another form of 'detachment', as though using it in ways similar to drugs or other sources of addiction, to escape from the frightening and troubling emotions of trauma.
4. A tendency to get 'lost in my own world' and withdraw from relating to others as a result of meditation.
5. A tendency to hear voices in one's head that sound like those of real people or to become convinced of ideas that are extremely unlikely or clearly untrue to other people. This refers to people who are at risk of disconnecting from reality owing to the impact of their traumatic experiences.[1]

If you notice any of the above as regular responses to your meditation practice, you should seek support in stabilizing them before embarking on regular meditation.

For most of us, working with traumatic and strong emotions within meditation is part and parcel of the practice. Even so, if traumatic memories do arise in meditation, the following tips might enable you to work more creatively.

Kindness meditation is a way of meeting these traumatic memories without getting overwhelmed and of re-experiencing the trauma as though it is happening again.

Attention can be directed internally or externally and have a single focus or an open-field focus. When we open the field of awareness, we discover more memories and feelings and can become overwhelmed, so perhaps we need to have more of a single focus, such as the breath.

An external focus is more helpful when we become engulfed by traumatic memories. Often our attention is drawn into the body, where trauma is stored, and so we can take our attention to the surface of the body, for example by connecting with a sense of touch. A rubber band around the wrist that can be snapped can help you to return to the present. Alternatively you could find a pleasant smell that helps you to 'come to'. You may have an essential oil with you in meditation that can soothe you. A fragrance with positive associations can help to shift your attention and settle your mind. You can meditate with an external focus for some or all of the session, for example using a candle or a piece of music to give attention to.

Once you feel more settled, you can gradually expand your field of awareness to include body sensations or labelling your emotions. You may move back and forth between aspects of your experience that help to ground you and those that are more challenging. In this way, when you are ready to explore your emotional experience again, you feel anchored (through the breath, touch, sound, or smell) every few seconds. This will aid in cultivating an ability to self-regulate as well as in developing emotional awareness.

If the formal sitting meditation feels too overwhelming, it may be helpful to do an informal practice such as walking meditation. Walking meditation can help to ground you while keeping you in contact with present external experience instead of getting overly entangled in memories.

Finally, if a trauma memory does arise in meditation, please do not feel you have to push through it with gritted teeth. It seems common in our experience of teaching meditation that people with a childhood history of trauma can approach meditation with an attitude of 'getting through it' and of working hard to do what they 'should' do even if that feels extremely painful.

We hope it is now clear that kindness should not be forced – it is a gradual, patient path. If you do feel overwhelmed, consider stopping your practice for a while. Most important, if you have doubts or concerns about your meditation practice and any trauma arising, please consult a qualified meditation teacher and/or psychologist.

If trouble does arise, have the confidence that your kindness practice has helped you already to develop some skills of emotional regulation and that perhaps it is time to seek further support in addressing trauma memories from your past.

Summary

If you know you have suffered significant trauma or even have a diagnosis of post-traumatic stress disorder, it is important to pick the right kind of meditation to experiment with and to pick the right time in your recovery to try it out.

Long retreats, intense long-term meditation, a view of meditation that is part of a philosophy of detachment, and the use of strong focusing of attention internally all have potential pitfalls for people with a history of trauma.

In the first instance, use this book to help you explore which practices most support emotional regulation for you, in other words which ones help you to feel most stable and secure and to regulate strong emotions from moment to moment. If any technique or practice is increasing your symptoms, making you feel dizzy, unstable, dissociated, confused, or falling apart, or is bringing up intense emotions that you can't deal with, stop the practice and choose another one.

Research box: A review of kindness meditation studies

Although more research has been done on the therapeutic usefulness of mindfulness, there has also been a growing interest in the possible benefits of kindness meditation. What does the research tell us so far? Shonin and colleagues systematically evaluated studies using Buddhist-derived loving-kindness meditation and compassion meditation. They found 342 papers and 20 studies (involving 1,312 participants). Participants showed improvements in five areas: a) positive and negative emotion; b) psychological distress; c) positive thinking; d) interpersonal relations; and e) empathic accuracy (that is, better able to recognize another's emotions and to communicate that understanding). They concluded that loving-kindness and compassion meditation could be helpful in treating a range of mental health problems.[2]

Appendix two

....

Resources

Further reading

The Heart by Vessantara, Windhorse Publications, Birmingham 2006

A short and warm practical guide to the five-stage kindness meditation practice

Change Your Mind: A Practical Guide to Meditation by Paramananda, Windhorse Publications, Birmingham 1996

An accessible and thorough guide to mindfulness and kindness meditation

Practical Buddhism: Mindfulness and Skilful Living in the Modern Era by Paramabandhu Groves, Muswell Hill Press, London 2013

A concise introduction to Buddhism giving the background to some of its ideas

The Art of Being Kind by Stefan Einhorn, Sphere, London 2006

Discusses the benefits of kindness and has a good description of true and false kindness

Why Kindness is Good for You by David R Hamilton, Hay House, London 2010

Especially good on studies of the effects of kindness

The Compassionate Mind by Paul Gilbert, Constable, London 2009

By the founder of Compassion Focused Therapy, it includes a thorough description of the three emotional-regulation systems

The Compassionate Mind Approach to Building Your Self-Confidence: Using Compassion Focused Therapy by Mary Welford, Robinson, London 2012

A practical approach to boosting your self-confidence with plenty of exercises

The Compassionate Mind Approach to Recovering from Trauma Using Compassion Focused Therapy by Deborah Lee, Robinson, London 2012

This book is a guide to working with post-traumatic stress using a compassion-focused approach and ideally would be used in conjunction with individual therapy

Authentic Happiness: Using the New Positive Psychology to Realize Your Potential for Lasting Fulfilment by Martin E.P. Seligman, Nicholas Brealey Publishing, London 2003

Best-selling book by the founder of Positive Psychology, the science of well-being

Classes and retreats

There are many places teaching meditation. Search online for meditation or Buddhist centres. All the centres in our tradition (Triratna) teach mindfulness and kindness meditation. To find your nearest centre, go to:
http://thebuddhistcentre.com/text/triratna-around-world

For retreats in the UK consult:
www.goingonretreat.org

Other online resources

For ideas, inspiring stories, and the latest research on kindness, see:
www.randomactsofkindness.org

The Compassionate Mind Foundation offers training, resources, and research into compassion at
http://www.compassionatemind.co.uk

The Mindful Self-Compassion website provides a range of resources and information to do with self-compassion at
http://www.mindfulselfcompassion.org

The Action for Happiness website has suggestions for simple steps you can take to be happier and other resources to do with happiness at
http://www.actionforhappiness.org

Appendix three

....

KBT research study reflections

This appendix is a summary of themes derived from our research evaluation of the very first KBT course. The course was still in development, so we were keen to understand how participants made sense of kindness as taught and experienced on it. The following excerpts have been made anonymous to protect the confidentiality of the participants.

Learning by doing; being an observer

All participants emphasized the practical emphasis of the course. They highlighted the benefits of learning how to cultivate mindfulness and kindness in practice via experiential components of the course: group work, meditation, and homework tasks that encouraged doing something differently. This theme encompassed a behavioural focus, suggesting that the course provided a 'learning by doing' framework that participants then used to clarify their understanding of concepts and ideas.

Here are Adam and then Linda on this theme.

What I appreciated very much was the way things were taught . . . : first experience, straight in, so basically learning by doing, and then the experience perceived was shared, then what it could have meant to different people was explored. Because you can basically try something out, experience for yourself, hear other people's experiences and then distil what . . . was good for you.

During the course I was thinking that it works because you come here and you apply the learning and you're doing it, which is obviously always much better than just reading about it, it stays with you.

....

One participant, Paul, commented on the structure and length of the course as promoting a more manageable commitment and focus to the course.

I think eight weeks is a really good length, it just brings a really good frame to it, so commitment and purpose.... apart from the theoretical bits, it's very practical.

Brittany connected the practical focus and the homework. She thought that the added structure of monitoring and reflecting on their course experiences on a weekly basis helped some participants to apply the course material more fully. This theme reflected an acknowledgement by all participants that mindfulness, like kindness to oneself and others, is an active process that takes practice to cultivate.

Hugely empowering, a fantastic practical tool kit that you can just take with you, very practical particularly with the research and science wrapped round it, the application of your own needs, and ... you can see benefits quite quickly.

Three participants talked about their improved attention to experience as like becoming an observer of one's emotions and thoughts. Michael emphasized this quality of learning to distance himself:

We explored on the course the whole idea about being an observer and ... distancing yourself from thoughts and/or emotions and ... observing all that and then noticing that you've got more or less control over or realizing what you're thinking.

Improved attention control and self-acceptance

All participants described a number of changes in how they related to themselves, including increased self-acceptance, decreased self-criticism, and improvements in emotional regulation.

All described a greater acceptance of the difficulties they faced in their life. This was particularly the emphasis of two participants, Carol and Michael. For example, Michael reflected on the change in relation to psychological symptoms such as anger. Carol emphasized a broader awareness of limitations in terms of strengths and weaknesses:

I suppose [I am] less judgemental in a sense of thinking it's OK to be angry to a certain extent. It's OK to feel depressed, but also thinking at the same time . . . that I don't always have to be angry, I won't always be angry, I won't always be depressed. So it's the combination of the two things: just being willing to accept it and being willing to allow it.

I suppose the first, the biggest step was in accepting. I think one of the points of the course was accepting when I'm not very good at something and accepting that I can't do everything and be everywhere and be everything to everyone, and just accepting things for what they are.

Four participants noted improved attention regulation and self-awareness in the moment. In the research literature, this could broadly be associated with the concept of mindfulness. In this instance, participants highlighted a greater ability to sustain attention in present-moment experience. This seemed to develop over the course. Thus Susan reflected that this increased awareness helped her to enjoy everyday tasks more:

Just doing something, being in the moment of doing it, rather than thinking I've gotta get this done because I've gotta do the next thing. It's like, I'm doing this job today. I'm gonna do it and enjoy it and see the results and not be preoccupied with the next task that I'm gonna do. The whole thing about mindfulness and concentrating on cleaning teeth and just little things like that, I always thought I paid attention to [them], but it's not even a conscious thing. Cleaning my windows the other week, I took ages over it and it was really therapeutic.

New meanings for kindness

A dominant theme that arose in post-course interviews was that participants developed a clearer understanding of what kindness actually entails. Participants such as Carol learnt to differentiate kindness from being nice to others, as well as honesty and a willingness to offer constructive feedback:

Kindness, that's not about being nice, that I found so helpful. . . . That session was probably one of the best out of the course, that kindness doesn't mean . . . always being nice and sweet and meeting everybody's needs. Kindness also means being honest and saying what is – not just feeding someone's desires or sorrows but also . . . saying look, I think this is happening or not just saying to someone oh yeah, you're right and that's really bad. Kindness also means supporting someone with constructive feedback. But . . . being supportive in an honest and constructive way.

Here Beverley and then Richard describe their change in understanding:

I suppose the recognition that I'm an OK kind of person and I need to learn to live or recognize my strengths and weaknesses and work with those rather than against them. And that's not a selfish action, that it's actually quite beneficial, I suppose not creating a barrier but being kind to myself in that, not putting pressure on myself to be there for people and not feeling bad about not being able to be there for them all the time.

That it's OK to take care of yourself and be kind to yourself and it doesn't have to be at the expense of being kind and caring to other people. It just has to be a priority for the latter to be possible.

Richard talked about being in the present and accepting his current bodily state as part of what he understood about how to foster kindness and Sylvia commented that kindness meant treating herself like she treats a friend:

Kindness can be applied or understood as being present to your . . . body, bodily conditions and just be with them. Basically saying it's OK, yeah? It's OK that my foot falls asleep during meditation or it's OK what's going on, so that's a level of basic acceptance, which is required for kindness.

I found that hugely helpful, that concept of kindness as thinking of yourself as a friend and therefore relating to yourself as you would do to a friend in need.

Making theory–practice links

In particular, the emphasis on what science understands about why and how kindness has evolved as a human capacity seemed to help motivate participants to explore the theories in practice. The theoretical components seemed to have had the knock-on effect of helping participants to test the theory against their own experiences.

Adam talks about his understanding of this dimension of KBT:

We explored giving and receiving, we explored gratefulness and appreciation, we explored what resists persists, the finger trap, all . . . underpinning getting some theory, but then the practice. People were given different approaches and then finding what works for us or for me. I think it's just something I really liked: the combination of theory and research, the more intellectual channel, feeding my brain something, I can think, and then, what it means in practice. It's this very neat combination of things, . . . something mind and body, relation, I think works very well for me.

Participants reiterated one particular theoretical point made about how kindness reflected one of three known emotion-regulation systems in the brain. This particular overview seemed to help them reflect on the complexity of human psychology and behaviour. Here are Linda and then Brian talking about their experience:

The sense that everybody works in this way, the scientific framework, I found really helpful, [it] just makes you realize your thoughts are not you and how the different brain systems go right back to our coding and can operate against each other. The three emotional motivators, was it? Yes, there was the fight or flight, then the next one, the addictive type mentality (goal/incentive-driven), where you're really going for extreme highs, then there was the third one, which focused on kindness .

I think [I have been] gaining a greater understanding of how we humans tick and the complexity really of how we tick . . . at the psychological level and then behavioural level, how our minds work and how we interact. How our connections work always presses a good button for me, and cements my motivation to practise it.

Gratitude and generosity

Linda talked about appreciating her relationship with her mother, and then Joanna, a journalist, reported she felt more willing to take an interest in others without expecting anything in return:

I think I'm just a bit more accepting of how she . . . relates to me. It's getting in tune with your own emotions about a relationship. So appreciation is very good at helping you . . . get a balanced view of an individual, but in terms of getting in tune with what effect that person has on you.

Taking a genuine interest, which I always thought I did. Actually seeing the person as a person and not a subject of my interviews, I'm so conditioned to get the story from this person that they are a story, they're not a person. So, just conveying the fact that I do give a shit and it's genuine rather than because I want something or it's a token gesture. I appreciate them more.

Joanna added how the course had affected conversations with family members and friends as well, similarly emphasizing a greater interest in what was important to them:

I structure our conversations differently, I've asked her [sister] questions that are more pertinent to her experience of things, rather than questions that I think are important to her, and actually listening to stuff that's important to her rather than brushing over it.

Liz stressed that taking a greater interest in others was reflected in an increased willingness to do more for others, to act more generously:

I feel more generous, more spacious, and more positive . . . more uplifted. I've noticed that I would do things, more things for her, really little things but I think they do make a big difference. For example, . . . if I cooked dinner, I would make the effort of leaving a note saying 'Here's lunch for you.'

Imagination

In particular, Michael and Linda referred to imaginative processes explored in meditation that helped them to manage interpersonal conflict in a new way:

With a difficult person I've started to feel much, much softer towards them ... using the light or imagining kindness all round me or my favourite place, or appreciation, or even thinking about what they are good at, ... taking a different perspective just helped see them with more empathy.

It [meditation] trains your ability to empathize by wishing various categories of relationships well, including in relationship with yourself, people you like, people you're neutral with or people you hate or you find difficult to deal [with] ... it practises your ability to put yourself into other people's shoes and therefore mediate your immediate needs with the needs they might have.

Common humanity

All participants reported shifts in their emotional response to others. And two participants described a pronounced shift in terms of greater empathy, a key competence in cultivating compassion, driven by the emphasis on common humanity. For example, Carol and then Richard emphasized the effect of the 'common humanity' principle and how developing self-kindness seemed to improve communication with others:

I suppose the realization that if you're kinder to others and more supportive of others, just feeling a bit more towards others, not so judgemental and a bit more empathetic, then actually things are a lot easier. Just the realization that everyone has something going on in their lives.

The facilitators were talking about people doing the best they can. That most people are always doing the best they can and that was a really novel comment because, I just thought, yeah they are. It might not be my best, but it's other people's best, and for me to criticize that best just undermines their whole being. I think that's one of the things that really came across in the course is the commonality of experience, on whatever level, be it good, bad or indifferent, but everyone's got something going on. It just really stuck with me about people's foibles and idiosyncrasies in the group and that actually we're all the same.

Participants pointed out that some of the exercises helped to facilitate taking on new perspectives towards others, in particular the concept of common humanity. Adam reflected on how the course helped him to see his overreaction to an individual he did not like much:

I now, probably thanks to one of the exercises [reflection on what a friend of an enemy would say about them], have a sense of well, he's not all bad sort of thing. OK no, I don't personally like him and I may find him difficult and so on but in reality, he must have some good points, he's not all bad. My overreaction I think is not often justified.

Changes in expectations of others

Changes in expectations of others featured as a theme in accounts of the course by Linda, Carol, and Michael. Similar to a sense of objectivity in a relationship, they emphasized seeing situations from different perspectives rather than just negative ones:

I'm feeling much more open, spacious towards people, especially more difficult people . . . much more . . . accepting, expecting less. Just focusing on what I don't like about them or what's difficult, the person . . . shrinks to just that, but I think the course helped me, really, to remind myself of in each person there's so much more, even those I don't like or have hurt me.

My expectations of people are more measured, because I don't expect anything from anyone anymore. And not in a negative way, I'm trying to factor in what people can manage, rather than what I expect from them.

I think a bit more forgiving. And possibly better . . . of acknowledging how other people make sense of split-ups and so on. Seeing their point of view, and letting go of mine a bit. It's not the end of the world, . . . it's not a . . . fatal judgement on me. If I do get something wrong, so what? It's that very sort of basic, not very exciting thing of just a bit more kindness to myself as well.

Chapter notes

Chapter 1

1 Matthew A. Killingsworth and Daniel T. Gilbert, 'A wandering mind is an unhappy mind', *Science* 330, issue 6006 (2010), p.932.

2 R.J. Davidson, J. Kabat-Zinn, J. Schumacher, M. Rosenkranz, D. Muller, S.F. Santorelli, F. Urbanowski, A. Harrington, K. Bonus, and J.F. Sheridan, 'Alterations in brain and immune function produced by mindfulness meditation', *Psychosomatic Medicine* 65:4 (July–August 2003), pp.564–70.

3 Shauna L. Shapiro, Gary E. Schwartz, and Ginny Bonner, 'Effects of mindfulness-based stress reduction on medical and premedical students', *Journal of Behavioral Medicine* 21:6 (December 1998), pp.581–99.

Chapter 2

1 Steven C. Hayes, Akihiko Masuda, Richard Bissett, Jason Luoma, and L. Fernando Guerrero, 'DBT, FAP, and ACT: How empirically oriented are the new behavior therapy technologies?', *Behavior Therapy* 35:1 (Winter 2004), pp.35–54.

Chapter 3

1 George L. Engel, 'The need for a new medical model: A challenge for biomedicine', *Science* 196 (1977), pp.129–36.

Chapter 4

1 Kathleen C. Light, Karen M. Grewen, Janet A. Amico, 'More frequent partner hugs and higher oxytocin levels are linked to lower blood pressure and heart rate in premenopausal women', *Biological Psychology* 69 (2005), pp.5–21.

2 Stephen W. Porges, *The Polyvagal Theory: Neurophysiological Foundations of Emotions, Attachment, Communication, Self-Regulation*, W.W. Norton, New York (2011).

3 Julia K. Boehm and Sonya Lyubomirsky, 'The promise of sustainable happiness', in *The Oxford Handbook of Positive Psychology*, eds. Shane J. Lopez and C.R. Synder, Oxford University Press, Oxford (2009), pp.667–78.

Chapter 5

1 R.A. Emmons and M.E. McCullough, 'Counting blessings versus burdens: An empirical investigation of gratitude and subjective well-being in daily life', *Journal of Personaltiy and Social Pyshcology* 84:2 (February 2003), pp.377–89.

2 S. Lyubomirsky, K.M. Sheldon, and D. Schkade, 'Pursuing happiness: The architecture of sustainable change', *Review of General Psychology* 9 (2005), pp.111–31.

3 M.E.P. Seligman, T.A. Steen, N. Park, and C. Peterson, 'Positive psychology progress: Empirical validation of interventions', *American Psychologist* 60:5 (July–August 2005), pp.410–21.

4 Philip C. Watkins, Kathrane Woodward, Tamara Stone, and Russell L. Kolts, 'Gratitude and happiness: The development of a measure of gratitude, and relationships with subjective well-being', *Social Behaviour and Personality* 31:5 (2003), pp.431–52.

5 Todd B. Kashdan, Gitendra Uswatte, and Terri Julian, 'Gratitude and hedonic and eudaimonic well-being in Vietnam war veterans', *Behaviour Research and Therapy* 44:2 (2006), pp.177–99.

6 Seligman et al., 'Positive psychology progress'.

7 E.W. Dunn, L. Aknin, and M.I. Norton, 'Spending money on others promotes happiness', *Science* 319 (2008), pp.1687–8.

Chapter 6

1 A. Lutz, H.A. Slagter, N.B. Rawlings, A.D. Francis, L.L. Greischar, and R.J. Davidson, 'Mental training enhances attentional stability: Neural and behavioral evidence', *The Journal of Neuroscience* 29:42 (2009), pp.13418–27.

Chapter 7

1 Cendri A. Hutcherson, Emma M. Seppala, and James J. Gross, 'Loving-kindness meditation increases social connectedness', *Emotion* 8:5 (October 2008), pp.720–4.

2 Ellen R. Albertson , Kristin D. Neff, and Karen E. Dill-Shackleford, 'Self-compassion and body dissatisfaction in women: A randomized controlled trial of a brief meditation intervention', *Mindfulness* 6:3 (2015), pp.444–54.

3 *Extravagaria: A Bilingual Edition* by Pablo Neruda, trans. Alastair Reid, Noonday Press, New York (2001), p.26.

Chapter 8

1 Marian Partington, 'Forgiving my sister's killers', in *Challenging Times: Stories of Buddhist practice when things get tough*, ed. Vishvapani, Windhorse Publications, Birmingham (2006), pp.9–20.

2 *A Blue Fire: Selected Writings by James Hillman*, ed. Thomas Moore, HarperPerennial, New York (1989).

3 Charlotte van Oyen Witvliet, Thomas E. Ludwig, and Kelly L. Vander Laan, 'Granting forgiveness or harboring grudges: Implications for emotion, physiology, and health', *Psychological Science* 12:2 (March 1, 2001), pp.117–23, doi: 10.1111/1467-9280.00320.

Afterword

1 James H. Fowler and Nicholas A. Christakis, 'Cooperative behavior cascades in human social networks', *PNAS* (March 8, 2010), doi: 10.1073/pnas.0913149107.

2 Martin E.P. Seligman, *Authentic Happiness: Using the New Positive Psychology to Realize Your Potential for Lasting Fulfillment*, Nicholas Brealey Publishing, London (2003), p.5.

Appendix 1

1 Available at http://www.jimhopper.com/mindfulness-and-meditation/cultivating-mindfulness/#caution-mindfulness-requires-readiness, accessed on 10 July 2016.

2 Edo Shonin, William Van Gordon, Angelo Compare, Masood Zangeneh, and Mark D. Griffiths, 'Buddhist-derived loving-kindness and compassion meditation for the treatment of psychopathology: A systematic review', *Mindfulness* 6:5 (2015), pp.1161–80.

Index

beauty (*cont.*)
  luxuriating in 129
  place of 125–7, 129–30
beliefs 25, 56–7
belly 13, 18, 49, 62, 172, 178
benefits 99, 101, 168, 170, 174, 176, 180,
    205–6
  health 31, 146, 174
benevolence 64, 127
benevolentia 64
bias, self-serving 100
biopsychosocial model 65
birthdays 72, 111
bitterness 165, 167
blessings 35, 95, 99, 101–2, 191
blocks to gratitude 100, 108
body 15–22, 29, 44–50, 66–70, 87–9, 150–2,
    170–4, 178–82
  awareness 44, 52
  dissatisfaction 150
  sensations 18–20, 26–7, 29, 36–7, 46,
    48–50, 62, 66–9
bonus meditations 7–8, 21, 45, 66, 68, 113,
    181
boredom 45, 136, 196
brain 56, 80, 83, 90, 173, 209
Brault, Robert 138
breath 13, 16–21, 29, 32, 48–50, 66, 87–90,
    92–3
  and kindness 87–8
  using 6
breath and body meditation 18–19
breathing 13, 17–18, 21, 66, 68, 87–8, 90, 92
  sensations of 66, 92
breathing space 66–7, 76, 92–3, 114, 140,
    161, 183, 190
  kindness 66, 75–7, 85, 91–3, 139, 182–3,
    188, 190
Brown, H. Jackson Jr 141
Buddha 132, 138, 164, 180, 185
Buddhist tradition 1–2, 91, 186
buddies 24

candles 23–4, 73, 89, 105, 113, 199
caring 73, 83, 158, 208
Cartesian worldview 151
caution 111, 120–1
CFT (Compassion Focused Therapy) 2
chairs 13, 17, 45, 73, 89, 105, 127, 147
checking 27, 132
chest 13, 18, 49, 178, 181
children 12, 19, 24, 71, 84, 103, 167, 170–1
choice 14–15, 20, 24–5, 40, 130–1, 138, 165,
    171
choosing 13–16, 25, 72, 131, 134
Christmas 108, 111
Churchill, Winston 108
colours 11, 15, 22, 50, 68, 85–6, 142, 167
common humanity 6–7, 141–2, 144–5, 147,
    149, 160, 166, 211–12

communication 87, 98, 131–2, 142, 151–2,
    155, 211
comparison 42, 104, 130, 132
compassion 2, 4, 40, 78, 84, 125, 145–6, 190
  cultivating 125, 211
  meditation 189, 201
Compassion Focused Therapy *see* CFT
    (Compassion Focused Therapy)
complexity 130–2, 134, 209
conflict 28, 64, 74, 81, 90, 106, 148, 156
consequences 57, 123, 145, 156, 158
constructive feedback 207–8
consumerism 3, 57, 83, 132
contentment 7, 77–9, 83, 85, 119, 129–30,
    134, 136–7
  care and, *see* care and contentment
  cultivation 133–7
  system 78, 84–5, 88, 90
control 28, 51, 101, 112, 133, 206
  loss of 81–2
control groups 104, 150
conversations 1, 10–11, 130, 152–3, 159,
    161, 210
core gratitude meditation 113–14
core meditations 7–8, 17, 46, 48–9, 66, 73,
    88, 105
courage 56, 58, 64, 135, 171
cows 123–4
craving 83, 132, 136, 165, 173
creative imagination 119, 122
creativity 58, 120, 193
cultivation of kindness 3–4, 7, 9–10, 55–6,
    70–2, 119, 185, 195
culture 3, 101, 109, 112, 146, 176
curiosity 9, 14, 40–1, 43, 48, 50, 54, 89–90
  friendly 68–9
cushions 17, 23–4, 73, 89, 105, 127, 147,
    178

death 17, 136, 143–4, 147, 197
deepening 193–4
depression 1, 5, 31, 81, 83, 96, 102, 104–5
desire 64–5, 121, 132–3, 136–7, 139, 144–5,
    157–60, 171–2
  nature of 132–3
  for revenge 169
detachment 198, 200
difficult emotions 40, 43, 46, 51–2, 58, 68,
    74, 173
difficult people 71–2, 74, 90, 106–7, 128,
    145–6, 148, 179
difficulties, turning towards 29, 33, 48–9
disappointment 9, 37, 51, 56, 133, 135
discernment 13–14
discomfort 15, 18–19, 25–6, 38, 49, 69,
    143–4, 173
  emotional 173–4
discontent 119, 130–3
dislike 2, 53, 70–1, 89, 112, 171
dissatisfaction, body 150

distance 41, 46, 59, 206
distraction 12, 47, 198
doing nothing 119, 136–7
downloads 8, 189
drive 10, 19, 77–9, 81, 83, 85–6, 145
drive 78–9, 81–3, 86

eating 37, 81, 97, 133–4
effort 10, 12, 29, 38–40, 62–4, 159–60, 173, 176–80
Einstein, Albert 100
Emerson, Ralph Waldo 185
Emmons, R.A. 102
emotional discomfort 173–4
emotional landscape 27–8
emotional life 5, 42, 54, 58
emotional responses 2, 5, 28, 152, 165, 211
emotion-regulation systems 77–9, 83–4, 86, 209
emotions 5–6, 14–16, 27–9, 51, 58–9, 66–8, 85–6, 169–72
  derivation of word 5
  difficult 40, 43, 46, 51–2, 58, 68, 74, 173
  knowing 84–6
  negative 46, 74, 106, 170, 172, 187, 195, 201
  painful 34, 47–8, 51, 107, 128, 148–9
  positive 59, 70, 99, 104, 112, 195
  strong 58, 199–200
empathy 31, 80, 122, 125, 211
enemies, near 53, 55, 111
energy 15, 36, 46, 95, 109, 120, 124, 176
environment 23, 63, 79–80, 87, 91, 134, 152, 190
evening 23, 75, 121
evolutionary psychology 7, 78
exaggeration 154, 156–7
excitement 77–9, 81, 83, 86, 88
exercises 6–7, 44, 46, 62–3, 67–8, 99, 173, 212
existential facts 143–5
expectations 3, 69, 75, 130, 133, 181, 195–6, 212
  changes in expectations of others 212
  lowering 75
experience 13–16, 26–7, 48–51, 133–4, 152–4, 171–2, 205–6, 209–11
  everyday 120, 176
  painful 38, 41, 48, 197
experiential avoidance 33, 36–8
  problems 38
extreme situations 163–4

false speech 154–9
family 19, 64, 103, 135, 142, 190, 210
fantasy 17, 85, 121–2
fear 39, 58, 111–12, 120, 142–4, 155–6, 167–8, 170–1
feedback, constructive 207–8
feelings, painful 50–1, 136, 165, 198

feet 13, 15, 17, 20–1, 44–5, 49, 124, 126
finest flowers 95, 97, 99, 101, 103, 105, 107, 109
five-finger gratitude exercise 103, 105
floor 20, 45, 124
flowers 23, 33, 53–5, 58–9, 109, 120, 164
focus 3, 15–16, 30, 48–9, 88, 91, 103, 123
food 81, 83, 97–8, 101, 109, 123, 125, 134
  junk 134, 156
forest of kindness 141–61
forgiveness 7, 163–83, 212
  benefits of forgiving 174
  benefits of not forgiving 170
  definition 164–6
  forgiving oneself 172, 175
  starting point 166–7
formal meditations 9, 18–20, 22, 44, 180, 199
fragrances 20, 164, 175, 199
friendliness 47–8, 50, 68, 89–90, 100
friends 69–70, 74, 99, 106–9, 127–8, 146, 148, 178–9
  friendships 42, 64, 81, 136, 159–60, 191
  kindness to 3
fruition 185–91

gardens 6, 22, 34, 55, 63, 120, 185
generosity 95, 97, 99, 101, 103, 105, 107–13, 115
  blocks to 111–12
  what to give 108–10
generous impulses 111–12, 126
germination 1–7, 33, 78
gifts 64, 72, 104, 108–12, 155, 166
goals 81, 83, 176, 209
Goethe, Johann Wolfgang von 139
goodwill 64, 159, 196
gratia 64
gratitude 6, 64, 95, 97–109, 111, 113, 115–18, 137
  blocks to 100, 108
  contacting 103–4
  diary 95, 102, 113, 115
  letters 102, 104
  meditation 105
  visits 104
great storyteller 43
greeting 16, 67, 181
grief 41–2, 163
grudges 163
guided reflections 7–8, 13, 44, 46, 62, 67, 169, 172

habits 11–12, 27, 34, 53, 105, 109, 136, 197
hangovers 37, 144
happiness 91, 101–2, 104, 108, 110, 131, 138–9, 144–5
hardened heart 168–9, 176
hatred 46, 71, 142, 167, 169, 187

WINDHORSE PUBLICATIONS

Windhorse Publications is a Buddhist charitable company based in the UK. We place great emphasis on producing books of high quality that are accessible and relevant to those interested in Buddhism at whatever level. We are the main publisher of the works of Sangharakshita, the founder of the Triratna Buddhist Order and Community. Our books draw on the whole range of the Buddhist tradition, including translations of traditional texts, commentaries, books that make links with contemporary culture and ways of life, biographies of Buddhists, and works on meditation.

As a not-for-profit enterprise, we ensure that all surplus income is invested in new books and improved production methods, to better communicate Buddhism in the 21st century. We welcome donations to help us continue our work – to find out more, go to windhorsepublications.com.

The Windhorse is a mythical animal that flies over the earth carrying on its back three precious jewels, bringing these invaluable gifts to all humanity: the Buddha (the 'awakened one'), his teaching, and the community of all his followers.

Windhorse Publications
169 Mill Road
Cambridge CB1 3AN
UK
info@windhorsepublications.com

Perseus Distribution
210 American Drive
Jackson TN 38301
USA

Windhorse Books
PO Box 574
Newtown NSW 2042
Australia

THE TRIRATNA BUDDHIST COMMUNITY

Windhorse Publications is a part of the Triratna Buddhist Community, which has more than sixty centres on five continents. Through these centres, members of the Triratna Buddhist Order offer classes in meditation and Buddhism, from an introductory to a deeper level of commitment. Members of the Triratna community run retreat centres around the world, and the Karuna Trust, a UK fundraising charity that supports social welfare projects in the slums and villages of South Asia.

Many Triratna centres have residential spiritual communities and ethical Right Livelihood businesses associated with them. Arts activities and body awareness disciplines are encouraged also, as is the development of strong bonds of friendship between people who share the same ideals. In this way Triratna is developing a unique approach to Buddhism, not simply as a set of techniques, but as a creatively directed way of life for people living in the modern world.

If you would like more information about Triratna please visit thebuddhistcentre.com or write to:

London Buddhist Centre
51 Roman Road
London E2 0HU
UK

Aryaloka
14 Heartwood Circle
Newmarket NH 03857
USA

Sydney Buddhist Centre
24 Enmore Road
Sydney NSW 2042
Australia

Life with Full Attention: A Practical Course in Mindfulness

Maitreyabandhu

In this eight-week course on mindfulness, Maitreyabandhu teaches you how to pay closer attention to experience. Each week he introduces a different aspect of mindfulness – such as awareness of the body, feelings, thoughts and the environment – and recommends a number of easy practices; from trying out a simple meditation to reading a poem. Featuring personal stories, examples and suggestions, *Life with Full Attention* is a valuable aid to mindfulness both as a starting point and for the more experienced.

ISBN 9781 899579 98 3
£12.99 / $20.95 / €15.95

Buddhism: Tools for Living Your Life

Vajragupta

In this guide for all those seeking a meaningful spiritual path, Vajragupta provides clear explanations of the main Buddhist teachings, as well as a variety of exercises designed to help readers develop or deepen their practice.

Appealing, readable, and practical, blending accessible teachings, practices, and personal stories . . . as directly relevant to modern life as it is comprehensive and rigorous. – Tricycle: The Buddhist Review, 2007

I'm very pleased that someone has finally written this book! At last, a real 'toolkit' for living a Buddhist life, his practical suggestions are hard to resist! – Saddhanandi, Director of Adhisthana

ISBN 9781 899579 74 7
£11.99 / $18.95 / €17.95
192 pages

The Journey and the Guide: A Practical Course in Enlightenment

Maitreyabandhu

'This book feels contemporary and relevant – full of situations and anecdotes that you'll instantly recognize from your own life. But it also goes deep. Being both practical and profound, it really is what it says, "a practical course in Enlightenment".' – Vajragupta, author of *Buddhism: Tools for Living Your Life*

How can you make the most of your life? Maitreyabandhu – a prize-winning poet who has been sharing his experience of practising Buddhism for over 20 years – sets out to answer this most basic question. With humour and profundity, mixing poetry and myth with down-to-earth instruction, he describes what it means to set out on the Buddha's journey and how you can follow it – day by day and week by week.

'The natural mode of consciousness is to expand. In every moment we can either allow consciousness to unfold or we can make it "me" and "mine" and feel it shrink back to the level of egocentricity. It's as if we've identified with a tiny ripple on the surface of the ocean. Once we let go of that identification *there's the whole ocean:* centre-less, edgeless, completely free.'

Maitreyabandhu is an experienced teacher and a member of the Triratna Buddhist Order. Ordained in 1990, he has written two books on Buddhism, including the best-selling *Life with Full Attention*, as well as two collections of poetry. He lives and works at the London Buddhist Centre.

ISBN 978 1 909314 09 2
£11.99 / $18.95 / €14.95
344 pages

Eight Step Recovery: Using the Buddha's teachings to Overcome Addiction

Valerie Mason-John and Dr Paramabandhu Groves

Human nature has an inbuilt tendency towards addiction. All of us can struggle with this tendency, but for some it can destroy their lives. Fortunately, recovery is widespread too. What can the Buddha's teachings offer us in our recovery from addiction? They offer an understanding of how the mind works, tools for helping a mind vulnerable to addiction, and ways to overcome addictive and obsessive behaviour, cultivating a calm, clear mind without anger and resentments.

'Through Buddhist teachings, personal experiences, and case examples, this book provides a wise illustration of the fundamental processes underlying a broad range of addictive behaviors. Mason-John and Groves offer here a practical and compassionate step-by-step guide to freedom from the deep trappings and suffering of addiction.' – Sarah Bowen, Assistant Professor, Department of Psychiatry and Behavioral Sciences, University of Washington, author of *Mindfulness-Based Relapse Prevention for Addictive Behaviors: A Clinician's Guide*

'Blending the MBAR program with traditional Buddhist teachings and personal stories, the authors give us a wise and compassionate approach to recovery from the range of addictions. This comprehensive approach will be a valuable tool for addicts and addiction professionals alike.' – Kevin Griffin, author of *One Breath at a Time: Buddhism and the Twelve Steps*

'The eight steps outlined here provide a simple, wise and practical approach to recovery from a wide range of compulsive patterns of behaviour associated with suffering. They provide a spiritual pathway to recovery for people from any faith tradition, as well as for those who are not religious, and for those who suffer from addiction as well as those who are simply aware of the suffering associated with the human condition. This is a book for everyone!' – Professor Chris Cook, Director of the Project for Spirituality, Theology & Health, Durham University

ISBN 978 1 909314 02 3
£11.99 / $18.95 / €15.95
264 pages

Not About Being Good: A Practical Guide to Buddhist Ethics

Subhadramati

While there are numerous books on Buddhist meditation and philosophy, there are few books that are entirely devoted to the practice of Buddhist ethics. Subhadramati communicates clearly both their founding principles and the practical methods to embody them.

Buddhist ethics are not about conforming to a set of conventions, not about 'being good' in order to gain rewards. Instead, living ethically springs from the awareness that other people are no different from yourself. You can actively develop this awareness, through cultivating love, clarity and contentment. Helping you to come into greater harmony with all that lives, this is ultimately your guidebook to a more satisfactory life.

1SBN: 9781 909314 01 6
£9.99 / $16.95 / €12.95
176 pages

Change Your Mind

Paramananda

An accessible and thorough guide, this best-seller introduces two Buddhist meditations and deals imaginatively with practical difficulties, meeting distraction and doubt with determination and humour.

Inspiring, calming and friendly ... If you've always thought meditation might be a good idea, but found other step-by-step guides lacking in spirit, this book could finally get you going. – Here's Health

ISBN 9781 899579 75 4
£9.99 / $13.95 / €12.95
208 pages

Living with Awareness: A Guide to the Satipatthana Sutta

Sangharakshita

Paying attention to how things look, sound, and feel makes them more enjoyable; it is as simple (and as difficult) as that. Mindfulness and the breath – this deceptively simple yet profound teaching in the Satipatthana Sutta is the basis of much insight meditation practice today. By looking at aspects of our daily life, such as Remembering, Looking, Dying, and Reflecting, Sangharakshita shows how broad an application the practice of mindfulness can have – and how our experience can be enriched by its presence.

ISBN 9781 899579 38 9
£11.99 / $18.95 / €17.95
200 pages

Living with Kindness: The Buddha's Teaching on Metta

Sangharakshita

Kindness is one of the most basic qualities we can possess and one of the most powerful. In Buddhism it is called metta – an opening of the heart to all that we meet. In this commentary on the Karaniya Metta Sutta, Sangharakshita shows how nurturing kindness can help develop a more fulfilled and compassionate heart.

Will help both Buddhists and people of other faiths to come to a deeper understanding of the true significance of kindness as a way of life and a way of meditation. – Pure Land Notes

ISBN 9781 899579 64 8
£12.99 / $19.95 / €15.95
160 pages

The Buddha on Wall Street: What's Wrong with Capitalism and What We Can Do about It

Vaḍḍhaka Linn

After his Enlightenment the Buddha set out to help liberate the individual, and create a society free from suffering. The economic resources now exist to offer a realistic possibility of providing everyone with decent food, shelter, work and leisure, to allow each of us to fulfil our potential as human beings, whilst protecting the environment. What is it in the nature of modern capitalism which prevents that happening? Can Buddhism help us build something better than our current economic system, to reduce suffering and help the individual to freedom? In this thought-provoking work, Vaḍḍhaka Linn explores answers to these questions by examining our economic world from the moral standpoint established by the Buddha.

'An original, insightful, and provocative evaluation of our economic situation today. If you wonder about the social implications of Buddhist teachings, this is an essential book.' – David Loy, author Money, Sex, War, Karma

'Lays bare the pernicious consequences of corporate capitalism and draws forth from Buddhism suggestions for creating benign alternatives conducive to true human flourishing.' – Bhikkhu Bodhi, editor In the Buddha's Words

'Questions any definition of wellbeing that does not rest on a firm ethical foundation, developing a refreshing Buddhist critique of the ends of economic activity.' – Dominic Houlder, Adjunct Professor in Strategy and Entrepreneurship, London Business School

ISBN 978 1 909314 44 3
£9.99 / $16.99 / €12.95
272 pages

Buddhist Meditation: Tranquillity, Imagination & Insight

Kamalashila

First published in 1991, this book is a comprehensive and practical guide to Buddhist meditation, providing a complete introduction for beginners, as well as detailed advice for experienced meditators seeking to deepen their practice. Kamalashila explores the primary aims of Buddhist meditation: enhanced awareness, true happiness, and – ultimately – liberating insight into the nature of reality. This third edition includes new sections on the importance of the imagination, on Just Sitting, and on reflection on the Buddha. Kamalashila has been teaching meditation since becoming a member of the Triratna Buddhist Order in 1974. He has developed approaches to meditation practice that are accessible to people in the contemporary world, whilst being firmly grounded in the Buddhist tradition.

A wonderfully practical and accessible introduction to the important forms of Buddhist meditation. From his years of meditation practice, Kamalashila has written a book useful for both beginners and longtime practitioners. – Gil Fronsdal, author of *A Monastery Within*, founder of the Insight Meditation Center, California, USA

This enhanced new edition guides readers more clearly into the meditations and draws out their significance more fully, now explicitly oriented around the 'system of meditation'. This system provides a fine framework both for understanding where various practices fit in and for reflecting on the nature of our own spiritual experiences. Kamalashila has also woven in an appreciation of a view of the nature of mind that in the Western tradition is known as the imagination, helping make an accessible link to our own philosophical and cultural traditions.– Lama Surya Das, author of *Awakening the Buddha Within*, founder of Dzogchen Center and Dzogchen Meditation Retreats, USA

His approach is a clear, thorough, honest, and, above all, open-ended exploration of the practical problems for those new to and even quite experienced in meditation. – Lama Shenpen Hookham, author of *There's More to Dying Than Death*, founder of the Awakened Heart Sangha, UK

ISBN 9781 907314 09 4
£14.99 / $27.95 / €19.95
272 pages